BONSAI
MASTERCLASS

PETER CHAN

Sterling Publishing Co., Inc.
New York

First paperback edition published in 1993 by
Sterling Publishing Company, Inc.
387 Park Avenue South, New York, N.Y. 10016
Distribute in Canada by Sterling Publishing
c/o Canadian Manda Group, One Atlantic Avenue, Suite 105
Toronto, Ontario, Canada M6K 3E7.

Printed in Singapore

This book was edited, designed and produced by
The Paul Press Ltd. 41-42 Berners Street
London WIP 3AA

Project Editor Sally MacEachern
Designer Jerry Goldie, Grub Street Design
Photographer Larry Bray
Art Assistant Claire Gilchrist
Index Margaret Cooter

Art Director Stephen McCurdy
Editorial Director Jeremy Harwood

10   9   8   7   6   5   4   3

ISBN   0-8069-6762-5 Trade
       0-8069-6763-3 Paper

Contents

Aesthetic and horticultural principles

As with any human endeavor, perseverance is absolutely essential if one is to attain excellence. The maxim, "practice makes perfect" is as true of bonsai as it is of music. You cannot hope to become a bonsai master just from keeping one tree – it takes years of experimenting with a wide variety of trees. Many people give up all too easily when their first tree meets with failure. This is a great pity as, very often, failure is caused by a lack of basic knowledge. Indeed, the tree itself might have been in poor condition when it was bought; something which the purchaser would not have been able to tell at the time. If only that person had been prepared to try again, success might not have been so elusive. This is why perseverance is so essential if you are to master the art of bonsai.

Perseverance alone, however, is not enough; you must love bonsai. In fact, unless you have a feeling for trees, you will not be able to sustain and develop an enduring interest in the subject. As with any other pastime, the fascination for bonsai is difficult to explain. Perhaps it is because the trees themselves are intrinsically beautiful. It could be the miniaturization, or the long time scale. But, at the heart of it all, is the fact that bonsai delight the eye. I have found that bonsai lovers invariably appreciate beauty, and that therefore they respond to the beauty of the trees.

Apart from perseverance and a love for bonsai there are two prerequisites for success: a sound knowledge of horticultural principles, and an understanding of the fundamentals of aesthetics. Both are vital: one without the other is of no value whatsoever. Good horticultural knowledge, without artistic flair, will not necessarily ensure the making of a good bonsai artist, while it is useless to have artistic flair if you do not understand how trees and plants grow. It

Many varieties of maple have been developed in Japan over the centuries, making them a favorite for bonsai enthusiasts, some of whom grow nothing else. This original wood-cut print by Kuniyoshi depicts an Ikebana master against a background of maple leaves.

盆栽

This 50-year-old Chinese elm bonsai is only 28cm (11in) high. The hollow trunk is an indication of its great age. Inspired by the beautiful trees on page 7, I am training it to resemble a typical old English oak.

is also important to remember that you are unlikely to create truly successful bonsai by mechanically applying the horticultural and artistic principles illustrated in this book; you also need common sense.

Understanding how trees and plants grow, their likes and dislikes, is all part of the process of mastering the art of bonsai. Some people seem born with green fingers: success with plants comes naturally to them. This ability will probably give them a head start and enable them to make rapid progress in their new hobby. However, gardening common sense can also be developed.

There are certain fundamental horticultural principles which most people will already know: for example, that trees can only be lifted and transplanted between the late dormant and early growing season, and not in the height of summer; or that trees only need to be watered and fed during the growing season. Nevertheless, throughout this book, I have assumed that what might appear obvious to some, will not be so obvious to others. In this way, I hope that the reader will pick up many useful tips.

It cannot be emphasized too strongly that the horticultural techniques used in bonsai are essentially those used in ordinary gardening. Thus, seed sowing for bonsai is essentially the same as that for commonplace flowers and vegetables. After all, seeds are seeds whatever form they take. The same is true of the various propagation techniques: taking cuttings and air layerings for bonsai is no different from taking cuttings and air layerings from garden plants. Grafting, feeding and pruning are no different either. Where bonsai does differ is in the aesthetics.

The right frame of mind

As you become more interested in bonsai, you may find that it begins to change your lifestyle: vacations, for instance, may include collecting expeditions, or visits to conventions and exhibitions in other countries, while your social life may broaden to include bonsai clubs, visits to bonsai conventions and master classes. This is all a natural development of the hobby and is equally true of other pastimes, as anyone who has taken up competitive sports, ballroom dancing, stamp collecting or bird watching will know. In time, the obsession with bonsai can become a passion. Indeed, it can become a way of life. You may find yourself thinking about bonsai every moment of the day, and probably even dreaming about it at night.

Enthusiasm alone, however, is not enough to make you into a bonsai master; you also need to develop the right mental attitude, or frame of mind. In addition to being interested in trees and horticulture generally, you must develop a critical eye for beauty, form and balance. Only in this way can you learn to distinguish a truly beautiful tree from one that is not quite up to standard.

Patience is of course a prerequisite: for while it is true that you can create a fairly presentable bonsai in a matter of minutes by proper shaping and wiring, it would take a minimum of three years to create a really exquisite bonsai, and it may even take a lifetime, or longer.

There is a sense in which the "perfect" tree does not exist, because perfection is always a question of individual opinion; there will always be someone who will find something wrong with any particular specimen. Nevertheless, this should not deter you from aiming for perfection.

Humility is another quality which the bonsai enthusiast will need to acquire. You will undoubtedly realize fairly early on that the Creator, or Nature, does most of the work; you can only lend a helping hand. When one sees a beautiful old tree in the wild, one cannot but stand in awe and admiration of Nature's handiwork. One is filled with a deep sense of humility, knowing that human beings could never create something as beautiful. In fact, one of the reasons bonsai appeals to so many is the sense of awe that these little trees engender.

Some describe this experience as empathy with nature; others as the awakening of the soul to the higher human sensibilities. Call it what you will – the fact is that bonsai does have some mystical or therapeutic quality about it that touches the human spirit. If it were not for this, the pursuit of bonsai would be an empty experience. Acknowledging the spiritual aspect of bonsai, however, will enrich your life.

Bonsai artists draw inspiration for their compositions from trees in nature. **Left** This massive English oak is 400-500 years old, and has a trunk diameter of nearly 3m (10ft). Although its trunk is completely hollow, the tree is perfectly healthy, and conveys an impression of immense character and power. **Above** This beautiful oak grows at the bottom of my garden – 24m (80ft) high and 1.8m (6ft) in diameter at the base, it is almost a perfect broom style tree.

Origins of Bonsai

In today's materialistic society, it is often forgotten that the origins of bonsai have religious and philosophical significance. Understanding bonsai in this context adds a further dimension to the pastime. Bonsai, like Japanese flower arrangements, are used to adorn the "tokonoma", which is the focus or shrine of a Japanese household. It is there that members of the family may meditate, or contemplate the beauty, serenity and peace of nature. The very act of placing a bonsai in the "tokonoma" is an act of worship with deep spiritual significance. A bonsai, therefore, may represent the deeper spiritual meaning of life.

The inspirational element

The fact that bonsai can inspire and elevate the human spirit is generally accepted by both enthusiast and non-enthusiast alike. The reasons for this, however, are more difficult to understand. One explanation is that bonsai trees are replicas on a miniature scale of beautiful trees seen in nature. Thus, if a beautiful piece of scenery can touch the human spirit, so too can a beautiful bonsai tree.

The corollary of this is that the inspirational element for bonsai lies in nature. Trees which inspire bonsai enthusiasts come in all shapes and sizes and can be found in many different environments. They may range from the large specimen trees set in the spacious grounds of stately homes to small, battered trees clinging to rocky cliffs. Whatever the setting, it is the image which remains vividly in one's conscious, and which in turn is transformed into a beautiful bonsai.

The process of creating bonsai is not a mechanistic one: bonsai cannot be created simply by pruning and wiring branches according to certain rigid rules and conventions. Instead, it is a long process which begins with an idea, born perhaps from a subliminal vision of a tree seen in its natural setting, and finally ending with the complete transformation of an ordinary tree, or plant into a spectacular work of art, which is able to evoke feelings of beauty, grace and grandeur.

As with all art, the bonsai is, in a sense, an illusion. The miniature tree is only the artist's perception of reality – a picture, or vision of the real tree. It is appropriate to compare bonsai with painting or sculpture: the creative process is sparked off by the inspirational element, the medium of expression is the living plant, and the final product is an image of reality.

The Bonsai tradition

Bonsai has been recognized as an art form by the Chinese and Japanese for centuries, and has been taught by bonsai masters for generations. However, in the West there is no such tradition because the art of bonsai is relatively new. Obviously, it will take time before this tradition can become truly established. As with all other art forms, practice is the key to mastering the skills of the medium.

The art of bonsai requires the right combination of mind, eye and hand. The mind needs to develop patience, humility and perseverance; the eye to become accustomed to perceiving images in a different way; and the hands must learn to shape and bend the tree into just the right line and shape, in order to inspire the viewer. All these qualities may take time to develop but, given the right guidance, the process can be shortened and, what is more important, made into a thoroughly enjoyable experience. This, therefore, is one of the aims of the book.

Left A rare example of needle juniper (*Juniperus rigida*) trained in the cascade style. This tree is about 60 years old, and is 55cm (22in) long, with a trunk diameter of 8cm (3in). Inspiration for the cascade style comes from trees which grow on cliffs, or on high mountain ledges.

Bonsai styles

Single trunk styles		
Formal upright		All pines, cedars, cryptomeria, larch, dawn redwood, ezo spruce, swamp cypress, Alberta spruce.
Informal upright		Most varieties; in particular, Japanese maple, trident maple, junipers.
Slanting		All the varieties used for formal upright are suitable.
Windswept		Junipers, larch, Scots pine.
Split trunk		Most varieties; in particular, flowering trees.
Driftwood		Mostly evergreens; in particular, junipers (needle and Chinese junipers).
Broom		Only deciduous varieties; in particular, elms, zelkova, silver birch, but not maples.
Cascade		Mostly evergreens, in particular, junipers, pines. Sometimes naturally occurring deciduous trees may be used.
Semi-cascade		Mostly evergreens, but some deciduous varieties lend themselves to this style; in particular, certain flowering varieties, such as wisteria.
Weeping		Naturally weeping deciduous varieties, such as willow; flowering trees, such as wisteria and laburnum.
Root on rock		Most varieties; in particular, trident maple and some junipers.

Exposed root		Pines, junipers
Planted on rock		Most varieties
Literati		Pines, junipers and larch.
Multiple trunk styles		
Twin trunk		Most varieties
Triple trunk		Most varieties
Multiple trunk		Most varieties
Root connected		Most varieties; junipers, in particular
Multiple tree or group styles		
Group or forest		Trident and Japanese maples, zelkova, Chinese elms, silver birch, larch, needle junipers, spruces (flowering or fruiting trees not usually suitable).
Group planted on rock		As above
Landscape		Most varieties, except large flowering and fruiting trees.

Aesthetic principles

Bonsai is now widely accepted as an art form, and not simply as a horticultural skill. As an art form, it has certain basic aesthetic principles which can be analyzed and studied. These principles are based on the aesthetic guidelines which shape all Chinese and Japanese art. Thus, in order to appreciate the aesthetics of bonsai, it is necessary to understand the context in which Chinese and Japanese art developed.

Almost all Chinese and Japanese arts and crafts have their origins in Taoism and Buddhism. Although complex and highly technical disciplines are often vital components of such arts, nevertheless they play only an instrumental or secondary role. The distinguishing feature of a superior work of art, or of a masterpiece is its quality of appearing uncontrived, or almost accidental. The highest achievement of Taoism and Zen (Chinese-Japanese Buddhism) is considered to be a man or woman who, without striving, is the source of these "accidents", or chance happenings in all the realms of art, including bonsai. It is these individuals who become the greatest "Masters" of their particular art.

Wabi and sabi

There are two fundamental principles which permeate Chinese and Japanese art and culture: the concepts of "wabi" and "sabi".

Wabi means, quite literally, "poverty", although this translation does not begin to convey the richness of its true meaning. Poverty, in this sense, means not being dependent on material possessions, rather than simply not having them. A person who is poor in these terms can still be inwardly rich because of the presence of something of

higher value than mere possessions. Wabi, therefore, is poverty that surpasses immense riches. In practical terms, wabi is exemplified in the contentment of a family living in very spartan conditions with simple food and few possessions, but surrounded by and in tune with the events of everyday life. In intellectual and artistic terms, wabi is found in the person who does not indulge in complexity of concept, over-ornate expression, or the pomposity of self-esteem. He, or she, is quietly content with the simple things in life, which are the sources of their everyday inspiration.

Sabi, on the other hand, denotes "loneliness" or "solitude", although in aesthetic terms, its meaning is much

Left Pictures such as this woodcut by the Japanese artist Umekuni are a rich source of inspiration for bonsai artists. **Far left** A five-tree group of 40-50-year-old Ezo spruce, which was once part of a much larger group imported from Japan in the early 1960s. The composition has been redesigned with the trees set slightly off-center, creating an asymmetrical balance, which is much more effective than a central planting.

broader. An antique element is also implied, especially if it is combined with a primitive lack of sophistication. The utensils used in the traditional tea ceremony of Japan are a good example of sabi. The essence of sabi, therefore, is gracefulness combined with antiquity.

To summarize: wabi implies poverty, simplicity and contentment; sabi, on the other hand, entails loneliness, solitude, some deliberate antique imperfection, and the absence of over-sophistication. Interwoven with these attributes are the innate qualities of a love of nature, preference for imbalance and asymmetry, avoidance of abstraction, intellectualism, and practicality.

In addition to wabi and sabi, there are seven other characteristics which are regarded as expressive of Zen in a work of art, and which link the concepts of wabi and sabi. These are: asymmetry, simplicity, austere sublimity, naturalness, subtle profundity, freedom from attachment, and tranquillity. While any one or more of these qualities may predominate in a particular work of art, all should be present to some degree, and should create a perfect harmony which characterizes that work.

Asymmetry

The majority of bonsai designs are asymmetrical in form and balance. Except in the case of the formal upright style, very few compositions need to be perfectly symmetrical. Harmony is achieved by careful balancing of visual mass and open space in just the right places and proportions (for example, the avoidance of opposite branches, or the subtle placement of the tree in a pot). The use of asymmetrical balance may be more noticeable in Japanese flower arrangement than in bonsai, but it is equally effective in both art forms. Stasis and over-perfection should be avoided.

Simplicity

In both philosophy and science, the most profound thoughts are often expressed in the simplest terms. This is equally true of bonsai, where over-ornate decoration of either tree or pot will detract from the design of the tree. The discipline of simplicity, therefore, is a vital aspect of bonsai design.

Austere sublimity

All surplus parts are discarded, leaving behind only the bare essentials required to convey the message of the artist. In bonsai, perhaps the best example of this quality is the literati style, where just one or two strong lines communicate the subtleties and emotions of the bonsai artist. A literati tree is very reminiscent of the brushstroke paintings of the literati school, where just the strong lines of the trunk and a minimum of branches and foliage can convey a richness which is based on a minimalist approach. The literati style is considered to be one of the highest forms of bonsai art. *Jin* and *sharimiki* (driftwood) are further examples of austere sublimity.

Naturalness

In order to create a completely natural feeling, the appearance of artificiality is avoided at all cost. The characteristics of nature are observed and copied in closest detail; the aim being to create an impression of the accidental or incidental. The result should look as if it is untouched by man.

Bonsai, by its very nature, is a man-made object, which means that a tree which is too carefully groomed may look almost plastic in appearance. It is vital to avoid such artificiality since the entire purpose of bonsai is to create "a piece of nature" in a pot.

ZEN AND BONSAI
The two fundamental concepts of Chinese and Japanese art – sabi and wabi – are linked by seven characteristics. Any one of these qualities may predominate in a particular work of art, but all should be present in some degree. The trees illustrated should point you towards learning to recognize these characteristics.

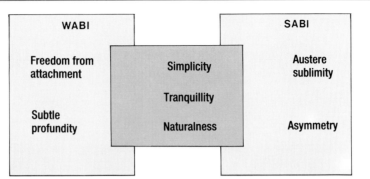

WABI		SABI
Freedom from attachment	**Simplicity**	**Austere sublimity**
	Tranquillity	
Subtle profundity	**Naturalness**	**Asymmetry**

Subtle profundity
Twin trunk trident maple

Simplicity
Common juniper

Tranquillity
Black pine

Naturalness
Chinese junipers

Austere sublimity
Larch

Asymmetry
Ezo spruce group

Subtle profundity

This is a very difficult concept to convey, but it involves intimations of inexhaustibility and endless reverberations. There is a suggestion of deep space implying some hidden ability or quality. It is easier to detect this quality in a painting, rather than in a bonsai, because depth and perspective are more clearly visible. Nevertheless, as you become more discriminating in the art of bonsai, you will begin to sense this feeling in certain designs. You may find yourself feeling a deep sense of respect for a particular tree. It could be the age of a tree which prompts this feeling, it could be its sheer beauty, or its regal bearing. Whatever it is, some trees are able to communicate subtle profundity in their own special way.

Freedom from attachment

This is characterized by the freshness which comes from abandoning convention, custom, and formula. It is only by adopting the unorthodox that one can achieve a freedom which is marked by freshness and originality. In bonsai, those trees which break the conventional rules are usually the ones which attract attention because of their freshness and unorthodox approach.

Tranquillity

This is another characteristic which is often associated with Chinese and Japanese art, where a feeling of deep calm, even in action, is conveyed by the subtle shades of an inkwash painting. Needless to say, certain bonsai also transmit this special quality of tranquillity.

Some trees are so noble in bearing that simply looking at them can impart a deep sense of restfulness and tranquillity to the viewer. Indeed, this is one of the reasons why the art of bonsai is pursued with such avidness in the West.

Personal inspiration

These principles may seem rather abstract and remote to the beginner, but in time they should become an intrinsic part of your entire approach to creative design. Translated into conventional design concepts they immediately become more familiar – line and form, balance and harmony, scale, perspective, color, texture, movement, and overall impression.

Keeping these concepts in mind, you should study the masterpieces pictured in commemorative albums and other bonsai books. By analysing the way these aesthetic principles have been applied, and by drawing inspiration from them, your understanding will grow, and with it your ability to create better bonsai.

Far left This split trunk Japanese mountain maple is considered to be one of the finest specimen trees in Britain. A small leafed variety of *Acer palmatum*, it is 90cm (3ft) high, with a trunk diameter of 11cm (4½in). The tree is almost 100 years old and much of its trunk has rotted away from the inside. However, careful management over the last ten years has arrested the rotting. **Left** This twin-trunk trident maple is unconventional in that the smaller tree is, in fact, a branch. The evenly spaced branches, radiating roots, and unusually beautiful trunk line make this magnificent tree appear older than its 40 years.

Choice of pots

Single trunk styles		
Formal upright		Medium to deep rectangular or oval pot; unglazed or dark colors for evergreen; unglazed or glazed for deciduous trees.
Informal upright		Medium to deep rectangular, oval or sometimes circular pots; color as for formal upright.
Slanting		Medium-depth, rectangular pot; color as for formal upright and informal upright.
Windswept		Medium-depth, rectangular, oval, or modern sculptural pots; mostly unglazed.
Split trunk		Medium to deep, rectangular or oval pots; colors as for formal upright and informal upright.
Driftwood		As for split trunk.
Broom		Medium to shallow oval pots (only rarely rectangular or circular pots); unglazed preferable; cream or light green may be used.
Cascade		Deep to very deep pots; square, hexagonal, octagonal, or circular; glazed or unglazed depending on variety of tree.
Semi-cascade		As for cascade.
Weeping		Medium-depth pot; shape and color as for cascade and semi-cascade.
Root on rock		Medium-depth pot; rectangular, oval or circular; glazed or unglazed, depending on variety of tree. If in doubt use unglazed, or neutral colored pot.

Exposed root		As for root on rock
Planted on rock		No pot required
Literati		Medium-depth, circular, square, hexagonal, octagonal, or modern sculptural pot; unglazed for evergreens; cream or light green may also be used.
Multiple trunk styles		
Twin trunk		As for informal upright style.
Triple trunk		As for informal upright style.
Multiple trunk		As for informal upright style.
Root connected		Medium to shallow, rectangular, or oval pots; unglazed or neutral colors for evergreens; unglazed or glazed for deciduous trees.
Multiple tree or group styles		
Group or forest		Shallow or very shallow oval pots; colors in unglazed, or neutral colored glazed. Flat pieces of rock may also be used in place of shallow pots.
Group planted on rock		No pot required
Landscape		Shallow, rectangular, or oval pots; preferably unglazed, or if glazed, neutral colors to be used.

Basic horticultural principles

The most important prerequisite for successful bonsai is probably a sound knowledge of horticultural principles. You must know how trees and plants grow in order to be able to manipulate them to the best advantage. Much of this knowledge can be acquired by trial and error, but hints and tips from experts can help you to avoid some of the pitfalls. The notes which follow are intended to act as guidelines, rather than immutable rules, and should be adapted to suit your particular local conditions. In other words, rely on your own common sense.

Bonsai soils

Bonsai soil is much misunderstood; yet it is perhaps the most basic horticultural aspect of bonsai. Some people plant their bonsai in soil dug straight from the garden, while at the other extreme, there are those who use nothing but pure artificial medium. The ideal, however, lies somewhere between the two.

It is widely accepted by gardeners the world over that soil which is too stony, too sandy, too peaty, or too clayey is not ideal for plants. In fact, sandy loam is generally regarded as the ideal planting medium. This implies good drainage and, at the same time, an ability to retain sufficient moisture. In addition, the soil must contain sufficient humus to maintain the vitally important micro-organisms, and enough plant food for healthy growth.

The general nature of these requirements means that their application can be subject to wide interpretation. However, essentially, a reasonable bonsai soil should consist of a fairly uniform mix of loam, peat and sand, with some plant food mixed in. The importance of good drainage cannot be emphasized too strongly, as the roots require air. The presence of coarse sand or grit in the bonsai compost should ensure good aeration.

A good compost, therefore, is a well-balanced one. The proportions of each of the basic ingredients, however, will vary according to the species of tree grown. Thus, pines and junipers will thrive in a compost which is made up principally of sand; rhododendrons and azaleas like a peaty compost; while

Bonsai soils

TYPE	TREE SPECIES	SHARP SAND/COARSE GRIT	PEAT	LOAM
General mix	Most varieties, particularly young trees	2	1	1
Pine or juniper mix	Young pines Old pines	4	1	0
Conifer mix	Cypress, cryptomeria, and other conifers	3	1	1
General deciduous mix	Deciduous trees in general	2	1	1
Fruiting and flowering mix	Deciduous trees which fruit and flower; willows; wisteria	1	1	2

The most impressive feature of this black pine (*Pinus thunbergii*) is its powerful trunk. The tree was imported from Japan and is reputed to be at least 100 years old. Its age is reflected in the gnarled, flaking bark, and the thick branches. Despite its excellent branch structure, the tree was grown for many years as a silhouette tree in the informal upright style, which meant that most of the branches had become extremely straggly. Over the last seven years I have opened up the structure, so that the two lower branches are clearly visible. In time, I intend to do the same with the upper branches. The tree is now 68cm (27in) high and needs repotting every four or five years.

flowering trees, such as wisteria and crab apple, prefer plenty of loam.

Experimentation, followed by observation, is the best way of finding out which compost mix is best suited to a particular species. If in doubt, a good basic recipe is one which consists of equal parts of peat, sharp sand, and loam. To improve drainage, increase the proportion of sharp sand; for pines and junipers the proportion of sand can be as high as 70-80 per cent.

The materials illustrated all improve the drainage capacity of bonsai composts: (bottom left) a typical bonsai soil mix; (bottom right) expanded volcanic aggregate; (top right) granite chippings; (top left) grit.

Fertilizers

All plants require nutrients in order to maintain healthy growth, and bonsai are no exception. In fact, because they grow in such a limited volume of soil, they require even more food than ordinary plants. The secret of feeding bonsai is to provide small quantities of fertilizer at frequent intervals, but only during the growing period – usually from early spring to early fall.

The fertilizer requirements of different species can vary tremendously. Evergreens, for instance, can be fed over a much longer period, i.e. from early spring to early winter in most cases; while deciduous trees should be fed only when they are in leaf, usually from early spring to mid-fall. However, all varieties of tree should be fed with a high nitrogen fertilizer during the early part of the growing season and with a low nitrogen/high potash fertilizer during the latter part of the growing season. This is a fundamental rule which should be applied without exception.

There are various proprietary fertilizers on the market in every country and it is unnecessary to list them all individually by brand name. All you need to know is that a high nitrogen fertilizer, such as 10:10:10, or even a general purpose fertilizer such as 7:7:7, is a good formula for use during spring and early summer; while a high potash fertilizer, such as 4:7:10 or 4:10:10 is best during late summer and early fall, as it helps to build up a bonsai tree's resistance to winter frosts. It is not advisable to use a high nitrogen fertilizer for bonsai after mid-summer, as this induces sappy growth, which in turn, reduces the tree's ability to withstand hard winters.

Tomato or rose fertilizer, which contains potassium and magnesium, is ideal for flowering species as it helps to set the flowering and fruiting buds on the trees. This fertilizer should be applied in late summer or early fall.

Almost any plant or tree fertilizer can be used for bonsai, so long as the dosage is reduced. As a general guide, all fertilizers should be used at half, or even quarter, the normal strength recommended by the manufacturer.

There are three basic varieties of fertilizer: slow release, granular or powder, and liquid. Slow release fertilizers are incorporated into the soil, and their use means that there is no need for any other fertilizer, although quick-acting fertilizers (such as foliar feed) can act as supplements to the normal feed. Granular or powder fertilizer is sprinkled on the surface of the soil so that it will leach into the compost as the bonsai is watered. Liquid fertilizers should be mixed with water at greatly reduced strengths. Never apply a concentrated liquid fertilizer directly. When watering a liquid fertilizer into the soil, it is a good idea to place the tree in a basin or large tray which will catch the run off from the bonsai pot. The collected fertilizer can then be reused.

Bonsai fertilizer regime

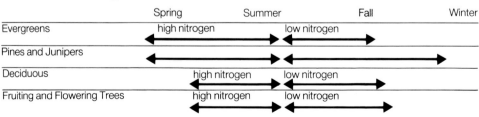

	Spring	Summer	Fall	Winter
Evergreens	high nitrogen	low nitrogen		
Pines and Junipers				
Deciduous		high nitrogen	low nitrogen	
Fruiting and Flowering Trees		high nitrogen	low nitrogen	

Chemical fertilizers are widely employed nowadays for all plants, and there is no reason why they should not be used on bonsai. Some growers, however, still prefer rapeseed and other organic fertilizers. These are fairly effective, but not as reliable and consistent as their inorganic counterparts. Nevertheless, organic fertilizers do possess one great advantage in that they release nutrients slowly.

It is preferable to apply fertilizer in the evening. First thoroughly soak the soil, then place the fertilizer on the soil surface and water it into the soil.

Watering

You may be surprised to learn that watering bonsai is a skill which requires experience to perfect. It is not simply a question of haphazardly applying a hose or a watering can to a tree: the frequency and the timing are both important.

The fundamental point to remember is that all bonsai must be watered regularly. This does not mean keeping a tree perpetually wet, nor does it mean relying on rainfall. The tree should be allowed to partially dry out before it is watered again, but on the other hand, it should never be allowed to dry out completely. If watering is neglected, particularly during the growing season, the tree could suffer irreparable damage. If watering is missed for even a day, the leaves can shrivel up. This is mainly because bonsai grow in such small containers.

During spring and fall, bonsai will probably require watering once a day in the evening. During the height of summer, bonsai should be watered at least twice a day – once in the early morning and again in late evening. Never water your bonsai in the midday sun as the combination of waterdrops and strong sunlight could badly scorch the leaves. During fall and early winter when the trees are under cover, you should inspect them regularly to make sure that they do not dry out completely. You should not water in freezing conditions; however, if watering is necessary, it should be done in the morning so that the trees will not be frozen.

Rainwater is ideal for bonsai, but it is not usually possible to store a sufficient amount for watering all one's trees. In general, ordinary water from the sink is the only practical alternative. If possible, it should be stored in large open containers to allow chlorine and other gaseous additives to escape.

Bonsai nurseries tend to use automatic sprinklers as a labor-saving device. The amateur, however, should use automatic sprinkler systems with great care since they cannot always be relied upon. It is far better to ask a trusted friend or neighbor to water your trees if you are away for any length of time. Alternatively, some bonsai nurseries will be prepared to look after your trees for an appropriate fee.

Use a watering can, or a hose to water your bonsai. If possible, rainwater is preferable, but water from the sink is perfectly adequate. I have been watering my bonsai with ordinary water for years, and the trees do not seem to have suffered any adverse effects.

Location

The placement of bonsai is another important factor in their success. As mentioned earlier, bonsai should not be kept indoors, unless you are growing a tropical species in the northern hemisphere. Even then, indoor conditions will never be ideal, for most bonsai need sunshine, fresh air and rain for healthy growth.

There is much debate as to whether full sun or shade conditions are best for bonsai. Basically, there is no hard and fast rule: it largely depends on the species, and also on local climatic conditions. Pines and junipers, for instance, enjoy full sun, while maples and other deciduous trees prefer partial shade. This can be provided by placing them in a position where they receive early morning sun, but are shaded during the afternoon. Shade netting is used extensively in the tropics to prevent leaves from being scorched and to keep plants cool, and serves as a useful shade alternative in other parts of the world.

Winter protection of trees is essential where temperatures fall below −4°C (25°F). In such circumstances, it is advisable to protect your trees by placing them in a cool greenhouse, or under display benches covered with glass or polythene sheeting. Drafts are highly detrimental to frozen bonsai as the wind chill factor can exacerbate the effects of the cold. It is advisable to protect vulnerable species such as trident maples, by sinking the pot or the root ball into a deep bed of sphagnum moss

A view of bonsai on a patio, showing how the trees should be displayed. The area is exposed to full sun throughout the year, therefore the trees should be moved from time to time, so that they get sun from all directions.

An example of bonsai staging which can be made quite easily by combining hollow concrete blocks and straight pieces of rough-cut timber. Tiered staging such as this adds interest to a display of bonsai by providing variation in height.

The hardiness of bonsai depends on the variety of tree, and on the local climatic conditions. In colder climates native varieties of tree will stand a much better chance of surviving the winter, nevertheless protection in a cool greenhouse is advisable.

peat. Evergreens generally benefit from some exposure to the cold: over-protection of pines and junipers, for instance, will induce sappy growth.

In very cold climates, where winter temperatures fall below −10°C (14°F), the more tender species, such as trident maples and pomegranates, should be overwintered in cool dry sheds or cellars. Light is not essential for deciduous species, but evergreens must never be kept in dark places for more than two weeks at a time or they will turn yellow.

From time to time, you should check the root balls of your trees to make sure that the soil has not dried out completely – they should always be slightly moist.

In Mediterranean and tropical climates, winter protection of trees is unnecessary. However, some species need cold conditions to induce dormancy and to enable the trees to shed leaves, or to produce flowers and fruit. If varieties such as Japanese maples, crab apples, larch and beech do not have cold conditions, they will be unable to go through their natural growing cycles, and will thus soon weaken and die. Many bonsai enthusiasts in places such as California, or the Mediterranean countries provide their trees with a period of artificial dormancy by putting them in cold store. Only in this way can the trees be induced to flower and fruit. Unfortunately, though, good fall colors cannot be produced easily by artificial means. Chilling the trees in cold storage might help – but I have never tried this myself.

Insecticides

Insect pests are as much of a problem for bonsai growers as they are for rose or chrysanthemum growers. There is no mystique to using insecticides on bonsai. Most garden insecticides are suitable, and the small size of the bonsai actually makes it far easier to conrol pests. To be on the safe side, you should use slightly less than the recommended strength of any insecticide spray.

Malathion is good for aphids such as greenfly, blackfly, and woolly aphis. It will also control many other pests, including caterpillars and scale insects. Metasystox is particularly effective if scale becomes a persistent problem (especially on trees such as needle juniper). GammaBHC is another good all-purpose insecticide, which will control many of the bark beetles and weevils. Insecticides containing fenitrothion are effective for controlling many of the moth larvae.

You should only apply insecticide once pests have appeared; it is not good policy to use it as a deterrant since insecticides can have long-lasting, harmful effects on bonsai soil.

Always spray in the early evening after sunset. Never spray in the late morning or early afternoon as the sunshine on the chemical droplets could burn and scorch the leaves of the trees. If it is necessary to spray newly-emerged leaves, use insecticide at half the recommended strength, or even weaker. Avoid using systemics as far as possible since they may have a detrimental long-term effect on your bonsai.

Fungicides

Species such as maple, beech, larch, cryptomeria, sequoia, and some of the pines tend to suffer from mildew and mold. Damp, poorly ventilated conditions in a cool greenhouse can be the cause, especially in the late spring and early summer. Any proprietary fungicide containing Captan, Benomyl, Zineb, and Maneb are effective for controlling both mold and mildew. As before, a weaker than recommended solution is advisable, regardless of brand. Unlike insecticides, fungicides may be sprayed at regular set intervals as a precautionary measure. If either disease appears, spray trees immediately with fungicide.

Herbicides

Herbicides are not much used by amateur bonsai growers as weeds are not a particularly troublesome problem. However, for commercial nurseries, herbicides are a boon, as their use can save a great deal of backbreaking labor.

Many bonsai enthusiasts display their trees on benches, which are usually on paved, or gravel-covered ground. Herbicides, therefore, are very useful for keeping these areas free from weeds. Simazine is a pre-emergent weedkiller which will prevent annual weed seedlings from growing.

If you are growing nursery stock in open ground, propazymide will kill off most annual weeds, including grass weeds and couch grass. If you wish to clear a piece of land prior to planting, glyphosate applied in early fall or early spring will ensure that the ground will be completely clean before you start planting.

During the growing season, annual and perennial weeds can be controlled by applying paraquat, which will kill off all the vegetative growth of weeds above soil level. Paraquat is poisonous and should be carefully handled. A hood should always be placed over the nozzle of the sprayer in order to direct the spray accurately and to prevent it from drifting on to other growing plants.

Regardless of the herbicide used, you should always wear gloves, goggles and a respirator when applying them. Never use herbicides on the soil of already-potted bonsai; always remove weeds by hand.

Trees suitable for bonsai

Botanical name	Common name	Botanical name	Common name
Abies species	Fir tree	*Laburnum* species	Laburnum
Acer buergerianum	Trident maple	*Larix* species	Larch
Acer campestre	Field maple	*Lespedeza*	Bush clover
Acer japonicum	Japanese mountain maple	*Magnolia* species	Magnolia
Acer palmatum	Japanese mountain maple	*Malus* species	Crab apple, and apple
Alnus species	Alder	*Metasequoia glyptostroboides*	Dawn redwood
Azalea	Different varieties	*Nothofagus* species	Southern beech
Berberis species	Barberry	*Picea* species	Spruce
Betula species	Birch	*Pinus* species	Pine
Buxus species	Box	*Pinus parviflora*	Japanese white pine
Camellia species	Camellia	*Pinus sylvestris*	Scots pine
Caragana species	Pea tree	*Pinus thunbergii*	Japanese black pine
Carpinus species	Hornbeam	*Potentilla* species	Cinquefoil
Cedrus species	Cedar	*Prunus* species and cultivars	Flowering cherries
Cercis siliquastrum	Judas tree	*Prunus persica*	Peach
Chaenomeles varieties	Flowering quince	*Punica* cultivars	Pomegranate
Chamaecyparis species	False cypress	*Pyracantha*	Fire thorn
Chamaecyparis obtusa	Hinoki cypress	*Pyrus* species	Pear
Cotoneaster species	Cotoneaster	*Quercus* species	Oak
Crataegus species	Hawthorn	*Rhododendron*	Rhododendron
Cryptomeria species	Cryptomeria	*Salix* species	Willow
Cydonia	True quince	*Sequoiadendron*	Giant redwood
Euonymus	Spindle tree	*Stewartia*	Pseudo camellia
Fagus species	Beech	*Taxodium distichum*	Swamp cypress
Fraxinus species	Ash	*Taxus* species	Yew
Ginkgo	Maidenhair tree	*Ulmus* species	Elm
Hedera species	Ivy	*Viburnum* species	Viburnum
Jasminum species	Jasmine	*Vitex* species	Chaste tree
Juniperus species	Juniper	*Vitis* species	Grape
		Wisteria species	Wisteria
		Zelkova species	Gray-bark elm

2

Humble beginnings: growing from seeds and cuttings

Many enthusiasts tend to overlook seeds and cuttings as potential sources for bonsai because they think that growing trees using these methods will be a painfully slow process, and certainly not worth the time and effort involved. While there may be a certain amount of truth in this attitude, nevertheless, in my opinion, it is misguided. In fact, growing bonsai from seeds and cuttings can be very satisfying, and need not necessarily be slow. Certain varieties of tree such as zelkovas, Chinese elm and larches are such vigorous growers that, from seed, they can attain a height of 1-1.2m (3-4ft) in a couple of years; their trunks, too, can thicken very quickly.

Attractive bonsai can be created from seed in a relatively short space of time by applying the correct techniques; for, to a large extent, the rate of development of seedlings and cuttings is determined by the way they are grown. Given the right growing conditions, a seedling can be made to appear older than it really is: a two- to three-year-old seedling, for example, can easily be turned into an acceptable bonsai with a minimum amount of shaping and wiring.

A typical cuttings bed at a commercial nursery: the glass frames, or dutch lights, protect the cuttings from bad weather.

Seeds

There are two commonly used methods for raising seedlings: seed trays or open ground seed beds. Each method has its particular advantages: while seed trays may be convenient and easy to handle, open ground seed beds are more suitable for raising tree seedlings since they can be left to develop for a year in the seed bed before planting out. Tree seedlings also develop faster and more vigorously in open ground conditions. Assuming that the seeds you have purchased are viable (i.e. they should either be fresh or have been stored properly), the treatment given to them

A crab apple tree grown from the seed of fruit collected in Kew Gardens, London in 1972 and sown that fall. It has always grown in a pot, and was wired into the informal upright style when about four years old. Aside from constant pinching, little else has been done to it. The tree flowered for the first time exactly ten years after sowing and has flowered every year since then. It is now about 38cm (15in) high with a trunk diameter of 37mm (1½in).

prior to sowing is a vital part of the overall process. Some seeds benefit from a pre-sowing treatment which encourages them to break dormancy, while others do not. A great deal of research has been done on this subject, but all the bonsai enthusiast needs to know is which varieties of tree seed require pre-sowing treatment: for instance, larches, Japanese black pine and zelkova do not usually need any pre-sowing treatment, while others simply will not germinate at all unless they have been treated. This pre-sowing treatment normally takes the form of a chilling process, and is commonly known as stratification.

The varieties of tree seed suitable for bonsai which require stratification are listed in a table on pages 42-3, together with details of the methods used.

Stratification

Stratification may be done in the traditional way by exposing the seeds to the elements, or by using more modern means such as a refrigerator, or freezer – either method is equally successful. To stratify seeds using the traditional method, simply mix them with sharp sand, or seed sowing compost, and place the mixture in a well-drained flowerpot. A packet of about 50 seeds could be comfortably fitted into a 13cm (5in) flowerpot; while in commercial nurseries large quantities of seed are mixed with sharp sand and placed in large clay flowerpots. The importance of good drainage cannot be emphasized too strongly; for if the drainage is poor, the seeds will rot.

The prepared pots of seed should be left in the open from early winter

To stratify seeds, sow them between layers of sharp sand, or grit in a large earthenware pot. Leave the pot outside during the winter; alternate freezing and thawing will cause the hard outer shells to expand and contract, eventually enabling the seed to break through. The seeds should then be sown immediately. More difficult varieties, such as Japanese white pine and hawthorn can be left for up to two years.

onward. They should remain undisturbed, exposed to rain, frost or snow, throughout the winter until late winter, when they can be inspected. By this time the seeds should have swollen sufficiently, and will be ready for sowing.

The stratified seed should be sown evenly in seed trays, or in open ground seed beds. The seeds should be covered with a 6mm (¼in) layer of sharp sand or grit, which will keep the seeds from being washed or blown away, as well as preventing birds and mice from eating them.

Stratification in a freezer is a much simpler process; it is also less messy. The seeds should be put in a plastic bag and placed in a freezer for two to three weeks; ideally in late winter. The stratified seed should then be sown immediately in seed trays, pots, or open seed beds at the end of winter, or early spring.

A third method of stratification involves using a refrigerator. In this case, the seed should first be soaked overnight in water and then placed in a plastic bag. Tightly seal the bag and place it at the bottom of the refrigerator. Over a period of about four weeks gradually move the moist bag of seed up from the warmest part of the refrigerator to the coldest part at the top (usually near the cooling coils). At the end of this period the seeds should have swollen sufficiently to break their dormancy, and be ready for sowing.

The varieties of seed which benefit most from stratification are: Japanese white pine, spruces, Japanese maple, trident maple, hawthorn, alder, field maple, hornbeams (*Carpinus* varieties), quince, cotoneaster species and varieties, crab apples (*Malus* varieties), and beech.

If the germination rate is poor (less than half), and providing the seeds were viable to begin with, it is probable that the period of stratification has not been long enough, and that many of the seeds should be left undisturbed until the following spring.

Seed trays and open seed beds

In my experience, seeds sown in open ground seed beds tend to grow faster than those sown in seed trays. In addition, you do not have to prick out the seedlings into individual pots during the first growing season.

Seeds which have been sown in a seed tray tend to outgrow their environment very quickly; consequently they benefit from pricking out into individual pots. This is best done two to three months after germination, when the seeds have put out three or four sets of leaves.

Seedlings which have been grown in open ground seed beds can be transplanted in the second year, and grown on in larger beds. The tap roots may be removed if desired, as this usually encourages a much better secondary root system. In fact, all the roots would benefit from a light trim at this stage. Regardless of the method used, all seedlings should be fed with a proprietary fertilizer during the growing season to encourage good growth.

Before sowing seed in open seed beds it is absolutely essential to sterilize the soil. The best time to start sterilizing a fallow piece of ground is in the early fall. First dig the soil over thoroughly and then rotovate it. Use a proprietary soil sterilant based on "dazomet" to treat the soil, and then cover the area with heavy polythene sheeting for two to three months. Just prior to sowing, take some of the treated soil and put it in a clean jam jar. Add some fresh cress seeds to the jar. If they germinate, the soil is ready to use. If not, wait a little longer and then repeat the test.

The ideal width for a seed bed is 90-110cm (3-3½ft), as this will allow you to work from both sides. It should be situated in a fairly sunny position, away from trees or hedges. To prepare the bed, dig it over until you have a fine tilth, mix sharp sand with the soil, add sterilant, cover the bed and leave it for two to three months. Test the soil in early spring. If it is ready, broadcast the seed evenly and cover with a 6mm (¼in) layer of sharp sand and grit.

These larch seedlings have grown to a height of 46-60cm (18-24in) in two years. The seeds were grown in a seed bed for the first year, then they were dug up, the tap roots were trimmed to encourage side roots to develop, and they were replanted 10-13cm (4-5in) apart in another bed. They were fed heavily with a high nitrogen fertilizer during the growing season, and the tops were left untouched.

can sometimes be one-sided.

Most cuttings respond well to feeding and should become quite vigorous plants in a relatively short space of time. Some varieties of tree, such as willow and pomegranate, can be propagated from fairly thick, old cuttings: branches which are as thick as 10-13cm (4-5in) can be struck.

Methods for taking cuttings

There are three basic methods for taking cuttings: soft material; semi-hard, or semi-ripe material; and hard, or ripe material.

Soft cuttings are struck during the early part of the growing season, using fresh, current-season growth, which is still green and has not yet turned woody. It is best to use the tips of growing shoots; ideally a piece of material with three or four internodes.

It is impossible to specify the exact length of an ideal cutting, as different plants have different internodal spaces: for instance, a trident, or Japanese, maple may have an internodal spacing of approximately 5cm (2in), whereas a dwarf azalea may have an internodal length of only 6mm (¼in). A trident maple cutting, therefore, could be as much as 10-13cm (4-5in) long, whereas a dwarf azalea cutting could be as little as 12-19mm (½-¾in) long. Thus, it is obvious that there are no hard and fast rules as far as the length of cutting is concerned.

Soft cuttings are usually nodal cuttings, while semi-ripe cuttings can be taken either with a "heel", or without a "heel". A nodal cutting is taken by cutting the material cleanly at the nodal junction, whereas a heel cutting is torn from the main limb of the parent plant.

In both cases, remove the lower leaves, and then dip the cutting in either hormone rooting powder, or rooting

This three-year-old Chinese juniper cutting (*Juniperus Chinensis*) is being trained in the twin-trunk style. The branches have been wired downward to encourage the foliage pads to develop; all branches are being kept apart, and not allowed to grow in the space between the trunks.

Cuttings

Propagation by means of cuttings is perhaps the most widely used method of growing plants, aside from seeds. Its greatest merit is, of course, the fact that plants grown in this way are identical clones to the parent stock. However, there are also some minor disadvantages: cuttings are not always as vigorous as seedlings and the roots

liquid. Now, insert the cutting into a seed tray, or a shallow flowerpot filled with appropriate rooting medium. This may be pure peat, a mixture of equal parts peat and sharp sand, expanded polystyrene granules, rock wool or expanded volcanic aggregate.

The secret of making successful cuttings is to keep the transpiration from the leaves down to a minimum. That is why it is important to cover the cuttings with either a propagator cover, or with a very thin film of plastic sheeting. Commerical growers use mist propagation, both to provide a humid atmosphere and to reduce transpiration.

Bottom heat helps to speed up the rooting process, although this is not absolutely essential.

The varieties of tree which are best struck from soft cuttings are: trident maple, all varieties of Japanese maple (including red maples), all the different varieties of elm, pomegranates, zelkovas, azaleas and rhododendrons.

Soft cuttings can root in as little as seven to ten days. If cuttings are taken in late spring, or early summer, they should have rooted within a month. The rooted cuttings can then be taken carefully out of their trays and potted up in individual 8cm (3in) pots to grow on.

Trident maples provide excellent cutting material. **Above** Choose a young tree that is growing well, and is free from disease. Select a piece with a large number of side shoots and, if possible, short internodes. **Right** When taking a nodal cutting, it is essential to use a sharp implement, such as Japanese scissors, or a scalpel. Sterilize your tools each time you use them, so there is no danger of passing disease from one cutting to another.

Above Ideally heel cuttings should be 10-13cm (4-5in) long with about four nodes. Pull the cutting material off the end of the main branch, leaving its heel intact, in the early morning or late afternoon. Plant immediately, or place in a sealed plastic bag.

Semi-ripe cuttings

The process is almost identical for semi-ripe cuttings. Nodal and heel cuttings can both be used, although the latter tends to be more successful. Rooting liquid or powder generally helps to improve the strike rate, but success very much depends on the variety being propagated. Most junipers, for instance, do not require rooting hormone, whereas Japanese black pines require very strong rooting hormone.

Semi-ripe cuttings can only be taken in mid-summer when the new shoots are just beginning to turn hard. Coniferous evergreens are best struck from semi-ripe wood cuttings 5-10cm (2-4in) long, and may be taken either in early or mid-summer. Junipers, however, are the exception to this rule, as small hardwood cuttings can also be used, in which case they can be struck during the fall and early spring.

Ideally, semi-ripe cuttings should be matchstick thin. Once rooted they can be potted up into individual 8cm (3in) pots in late summer to grow on. If cuttings are taken in late summer, they should not be disturbed until the following spring or summer, otherwise you may break the roots, or even kill the young plant.

Cuttings from most varieties of evergreen can be taken at virtually any time of year; heel cuttings, however, are more successful than nodal cuttings. They should be 5-10cm (2-4in) long, and the wood should be semi-hard.

Cuttings can be planted in open ground beds with a high proportion of sand, but trays are easier to handle. Do not fertilize until the roots are fully developed, and keep the cuttings in a cool greenhouse, or a sheltered spot for six months.

Hardwood cuttings

As with semi-ripe cuttings, hardwood cuttings are best taken with a heel; but whereas semi-ripe cuttings are taken in the summer, hardwood cuttings are taken in the fall. Both types are best propagated without bottom heat.

Commercial nurseries strike hardwood and semi-ripe cuttings in frames, or dutch lights (a glazed frame set in a brick or wooden framework). During the summer, the covers of these frames are draped with some form of shading, such as reed mats, to prevent them from being scorched by the sun, and to keep the cuttings cool.

All types of cutting should be watered regularly so that they do not dry out. Roots may be produced in as little as two weeks. Once the cuttings have rooted, more light can be introduced gradually to accelerate their growth. As with seedlings, you do not have to raise them in seed beds, although this is more convenient, but in specially prepared beds in the frames, or dutch lights.

After the first few months, pot evergreen cuttings individually, and fertilize heavily. In the second year, plant them in an open bed, continue fertilizing, and spray if you see pests. **Above** This two-year-old Chinese juniper is ideal raw material for creating a bonsai. **left** An 18cm (7in) two-year-old seedling trained in the twin-trunk style. Wiring will encourage the trunks to curve gently, and the branches to spread laterally.

These propagating beds should be prepared a couple of months before use, in the same way as seed beds, by sterilizing the soil with any of the proprietary sterilants. This will kill off any weed seeds and roots, which are lying dormant in the bed, thus ensuring that the cuttings will grow unimpeded. The sterilized soil should be mixed with generous quantities of coarse grit, or sharp sand in order to provide good drainage, and ensure a naturally open mix. It is, of course, not necessary to use bottom heat with cutting beds.

Not many varieties of tree used for bonsai can be successfully propagated from hardwood cuttings, with the exception of deciduous trees such as poplars and willows. The latter root so readily that very thick cuttings can be taken at any time of year, although spring and summer are best. Zelkova, Chinese elm, and trident maples can be struck in the early spring from hardwood cuttings up to 13cm (1/2in) thick; bottom heat, however, must be used.

An eight-year-old
Japanese gray-bark elm
(*Zelkova*), developed
from the seedling shown
on the opposite page
(top), and trained in the
broom style.

Developing Bonsai from seedlings and cuttings

Producing seedlings and cuttings is only
a tiny, albeit important, part of the total
bonsai process. After all, seedlings and
cuttings are just raw material, which
requires training before it can be
considered to be a bonsai.

One of the first decisions you need to
make concerns the dimensions of the
intended bonsai: the eventual height and
trunk thickness of the tree will govern the
way you develop the seedling or cutting.

Two- to three-year-old cuttings or
seedlings make good small bonsai: they
will probably be no higher than 20-23cm
(8-9in), with trunks approximately
6-13mm (¼-½in) thick. The size of the
trunk depends on the variety, and also
on how the trees have been grown.
Cuttings and seedlings which have been
grown vigorously in the open ground will
have thicker trunks than those grown in
seed trays, although seedlings and

cuttings which have been potted on in progressively larger pots could attain the same vigor. Trident maples, Chinese elm, and zelkova are particularly vigorous varieties, and if left undisturbed to grow in open ground with plenty of light, fertilizer and water, they can develop trunks of up to 50mm (2in) or more, and a height of 3-3.7m (10-12ft) in five years.

Techniques for developing Bonsai

Many people are introduced to bonsai through attractively packaged bonsai seed kits which contain a few tree seeds and a small pot of soil. Seed kits can be fun, and provided the seeds are viable, a fair proportion should germinate to become potential bonsai material. However, raising seeds successfully is only the first step in making bonsai; the seedlings will need to be properly trained and shaped if they are to become artistic trees. If seedlings are left to develop without any training whatsoever they merely end up as very ordinary nursery material. It is not surprising, therefore, that most beginners do not know how to proceed once the seedlings have germinated, which leads to disappointment, and often to the abandonment of bonsai as a hobby. This is a great pity, and can easily be avoided.

There are two basic ways of developing bonsai from seedlings and cuttings. The first is an age-old method which has been practiced by the Chinese for centuries. It is known as the "clip and grow" method, and involves constant clipping and cutting back until the desired shape is achieved. The second method has been developed more recently, and involves using wire to bend the tree into the desired shape. Both these methods are described in more detail on the following pages.

The Japanese gray-bark elm is one of the most popular varieties of tree for bonsai, and is certainly one of the easiest to germinate. **Above** and **below** These two-year-old seedlings are approximately 20cm (8in) high, and illustrate the two variants of broom style.

Clip and grow method

The newly-germinated seedlings, or freshly struck cuttings, should be allowed to grow strongly for the first two years so that the trunks can thicken. Some bonsai growers in Japan meticulously examine the roots of the young plants, removing the tap root and any vigorous side roots in order to ensure that a good radial root system is developed right from the start. The amateur may wish to do the same, but at this stage, the priority is to encourage the seedlings to grow vigorously.

The seedlings may be grown in specially prepared nursery beds (*see p31*) or in a flowerpot. They should be fertilized quite heavily during the growing season for the first two years. If the young plants have been grown well they should attain a height of between 30-90cm (12-36in), depending on the species: maples, for instance, can grow to 46cm (18in) in two years, while zelkovas and Chinese elms can reach a height of 90cm (3ft) in two years from seed. However, the objective is not to let the trees grow excessively tall, but to develop a small, compact tree so that the trunk thickness is in proportion to the finished bonsai.

The best time to begin training a young tree is when it is about two years old. If it is any younger the tree will not have developed sufficiently, and if it is older the trunk may have become too stiff to be shaped. When a seedling has reached the desired height and thickness of trunk, it should be dug out of the ground and placed in a flowerpot, or a small seed tray. The seedlings may be planted singly, in pairs, or even as many as 3-5 to a flowerpot. The compost used for young seedlings is not particularly important, as long as it is well drained, since the main nourishment for the plants will be provided by fertilizers.

Most cuttings are taken when small and slender, with the exception of varieties such as willows and pomegranates. This 18cm (7in) thick willow cutting was actually part of a trunk. It was planted in early spring in a flowerpot of sharp sand and placed in a shallow tray of water. The cutting was repotted in compost after three months, and only fed once the roots were well-established.

After replanting the seedlings, allow them to grow uninhibited for a year, increasing in height and trunk thickness. In the spring of the following year, cut the young seedlings back to half their original height, retaining only one or two nodes of the current season's growth. After this drastic pruning, allow the tree to grow without restrictions for another year: a new leader should develop, together with some new side branches.

In the following spring (i.e. in the fifth year), repeat the process, cutting off all the previous season's growth with the exception of two or three nodes. If side branches have grown, these too should be clipped back to encourage dense bushy branch development. At this stage the tree should be dug up, the roots

This cutting, taken from a weeping willow three years ago, already has a 15cm (6in) diameter trunk, and is thus well on its way to becoming a fine bonsai.

By taking a branch from an established tree, this zelkova cutting began life with wood that was already four years old. It was propagated using bottom heat and rooted in about six weeks. Four months later, it is quite an acceptable little bonsai.

should be pruned, and the tree replanted in the training pot or seed tray.

This process of cutting all growth back to two or three nodes of the current season's growth should be repeated every year until the tree is about eight to ten years old. The roots only need to be pruned every other year. By this time the young sapling should have attained a pleasing taper, and also a sizable trunk.

Using this method of training seedlings and cuttings, most bonsai should reach a height of about 30-38cm (12-15in) and a trunk diameter of 25-48mm (1-1½in). "Clip and grow" training is undoubtedly a tedious process, but very fine, well-formed bonsai can be produced this way. There are, of course, quicker ways of developing trees with much thicker trunks which are explained in later chapters. It is extremely satisfying, however, to own bonsai which you have shaped and trained yourself.

Wiring method

As with the "cut and grow" method, you start with two-year-old seedlings and cuttings. The roots may be trimmed back before potting on in training pots, or planting in a growing bed. The most important process however is the wiring of the trunk into a gentle "S" curve. This is an absolutely crucial operation since it determines the final shape of the tree for the rest of its life as a bonsai (*see p84-5*). Once the tree is wired it can be replanted in the ground or in a large flowerpot, and left to grow for the next two years.

During these two years (the third and fourth year of growth) the only training needed is constant pinching so that the branches form dense twigs, allowing all the goodness (i.e. plant cell development) to go into the main trunk. As a result, the trunk should thicken quite considerably, and at the end of the two year period, the tree can be dug up for root pruning and repotting.

The roots should be trimmed so that they are all of uniform length and spreading out radially. There is no need to select the final side branches to be retained, as this can be left to a later stage. The main objective during the initial growing period is to encourage a large number of dense branches to form along the trunk by constantly pinching their tips.

After the first two years of training, the wire should be removed to prevent it from marking the tree excessively. The longer branches should be trimmed back. If the growing tips are stopped, side shoots will be encouraged to form. In turn, if the side shoots are stopped, they will develop further side shoots, thus encouraging the formation of dense, twiggy growth. The tree should be root pruned and repotted after the fourth year.

Allow the tree to grow uninhibited, except for constant pinching, during the fifth and sixth year. After the sixth year the tree should be root pruned again and repotted – either in a training pot, or a proper bonsai pot.

By the seventh year the branches for the final bonsai design should be chosen and the unwanted branches removed. Constant stopping and pinching of the remaining branches should produce a dense, twiggy branch formation, and by the time the tree is eight years old it should be a credible-looking bonsai.

Right A four-year-old Japanese larch seedling (*Larix kaempferi*), which has been grown in an open ground seed bed. At a height of 1m (3ft), and with a trunk diameter of 19mm (¾in), it is ready for shaping into a bonsai. **Above** One hour later, and the seedling is transformed: the top 30cm (1ft) has been removed; a side branch has become the new leader; and the trunk has been wired, as have selected, evenly-spaced branches, giving the tree a conical shape.

Developed from seed, this larch is only 15 years old, and is 43cm (17in) high with a 5cm (2in) trunk. The striking driftwood effect has been created by stripping the trunk bare. The unglazed, oval pot has been chosen to create a contrast between its soft coloring and the rugged style of the tree.

41

Final points

With both methods of training bonsai, the secret is regular feeding during the growing season to encourage healthy, vigorous growth. In addition, with wired bonsai, constant pinching is necessary to develop density and fine branch formation. Only when the tree has reached a reasonable height, should you begin the final refinement of the tree as a bonsai.

The cutting back method is particularly suitable for very vigorous deciduous trees. Evergreens, on the other hand, do not produce new branches as readily as deciduous trees, thus making them less suitable material for the "clip and grow" method. However, both deciduous and evergreen trees may be wired into their final shapes, such as the classic "S" shape, from a very early age and left to develop in the ground.

In both cases, it is important to have a fairly clear idea of the size of the bonsai you wish to create, so that the tree can be stopped at the desired height. It would obviously be a mistake to design a 15cm (6in) tree and then hope it will develop successfuly into a large 60cm (2ft) tree over a long period of time. If the object is to create a small tree, then this should be your aim from the very beginning. In the same way, a large tree

SEEDS REQUIRING STRATIFICATION

Abies species	Stratify in sand for 6 weeks, or chill in freezer for 3 weeks.
Acer buergerianum (trident maple)	Stratify in sand for 8 weeks, or chill in freezer for 4 weeks.
Acer campestre (field maple)	Stratify in sand for 8 weeks, or chill in freezer for 4 weeks.
Acer ginnala (Amur maple)	Stratify in sand for 8 weeks, or chill in freezer for 4 weeks.
Acer japonicum (Japanese mountain maple)	Stratify in sand for 8 weeks, or chill in freezer for 4 weeks.
Acer palmatum (Japanese mountain maple)	Stratify in sand for 8 weeks, or chill in freezer for 4 weeks.
Alnus species (alder)	Chill in freezer for 2 weeks.
Berberis species (barberry)	Stratify in sand for 6-8 weeks, or chill in freezer for 3-4 weeks.
Betula species (birch)	Chill in freezer for 2-4 weeks.
Camellia species	Chill in fridge for 2 weeks.
Carpinus species (hornbeam)	Stratify in sand for 8-12 weeks, or chill in freezer for 3-4 weeks.
Cotoneaster species	Stratify in sand for 6-8 weeks, or chill in freezer for 3-4 weeks.
Crataegus species (hawthorn)	Stratify for at least 8 weeks in sand, or over 2 winters. (May also be chilled in freezer for 4 weeks, taking them out to thaw every other week.)
Cydonia (true quince)	Sow immediately after collection. Otherwise stratify in sand for 4 weeks.
Euonymus (spindle tree)	Stratify in sand for 8-12 weeks, or chill in freezer for 6-8 weeks.
Fagus species (beech)	Stratify in sand for 6-8 weeks, or chill in freezer for 6-8 weeks.
Juniperus species	Stratify in sand for 4-6 weeks, or chill in freezer for 2-3 weeks.

is usually trained with that specific objective in mind right from the start.

Producing a large bonsai from a seed or cutting requires time and infinite patience. The tree would need to be constantly pinched, wired and trimmed over a period of many years (30-40 perhaps), while the trunk and branches thickened gradually. Some of the finest bonsai in Japan have been produced using this method, which is sometimes known as the "growing-up" method, as opposed to the "growing-down" or quick method, where large trees are chopped down to the desired height and their branches regrown.

Seedlings and cuttings, therefore, are viable means of producing bonsai of all shapes and sizes. The process can be either quick or slow: the rate of development depends entirely on the growing conditions provided, and is used commercially on a large scale in both China and Japan as it is both quick and cheap. There is no real mystique to raising seedlings and cuttings, the difficult part is learning how to turn them into attractive bonsai. This requires applying a combination of aesthetic principles, horticultural skills, and special techniques. Although this may sound daunting, especially to the beginner, all you need is practice – you will then find that what seemed difficult is in fact easy.

Laburnum	No stratification needed, but germination could be improved by pouring boiling water over the seeds just prior to sowing.
Larix species (larch)	Chill in fridge for 2 weeks only. However, stratification is not really necessary.
Lespedeza (bush clover)	Chill in freezer for 2 weeks.
Malus species (crab apple)	Sow immediately after collecting fruit in fall. Stored seed should be stratified in sand for 4-6 weeks, or in freezer for 2-3 weeks
Nothofagus species (southern beech)	Chill in freezer for 6-8 weeks.
Pinus species (most pines)	Stratify in sand for 4-6 weeks, or chill in freezer for 2-3 weeks, except the following:
Pinus parviflora (Japanese white pine)	Stratify in sand for 8-12 weeks, or chill in freezer for 4-6 weeks.
Prunus species and cultivars (cherries)	Stratify in sand for 8-12 weeks, or chill in freezer for 4-6 weeks.
Pyracantha	Stratify in sand for 4-6 weeks, or chill in freezer for 2-3 weeks.
Rhododendron	Chill in freezer for 2-3 weeks.
Sequoiadendron	Stratify in sand for 4-6 weeks, or chill in freezer for 2-3 weeks.
Stewartia	Chill in fridge for 2-3 weeks.
Taxus species (yews)	Very long stratification in sand for up to 2 years.
Vitex species (chaste tree)	Chill in freezer for 2-4 weeks.

3 Shortening the time scale

The time scales in bonsai are long: the process of creating an attractive tree can take decades. You have to think in terms of years and growing seasons rather than in months and days. In a sense this is very much part of the Oriental tradition, where people accept that certain things just cannot be hurried. Patience is regarded as a cardinal virtue; there is seldom any resentment at having to wait. This is particularly true of bonsai: waiting for a tree to mature is part of the enjoyment – there is tremendous satisfaction in growing old with one's trees. Old bonsai become heirlooms which are passed on from one generation to the next.

In recent years values have changed, largely as a result of Western influence, and there has been a noticeable move away from the veneration of age. Increasingly, people are taught to regard the age of a tree as being of secondary importance to its beauty. Nevertheless, despite this trend, age remains one of the most important intrinsic qualities of a bonsai. One of the most frequent questions asked at horticultural shows where bonsai are exhibited is: "How old is that tree?" There is often a disappointed reaction if a particular tree is not as old as the viewer expected it to be.

There is something special about a very old tree. Apart from the mystique, age is often one of the main factors which distinguishes a masterpiece from an ordinary bonsai. As with antiques, age imparts a certain quality and feel that can only be appreciated by the viewer; it is not something which can be described in so many words.

It is human nature, however, to be impatient, which means that most people will try to take shortcuts to achieve their aims. This desire to save time and energy is not necessarily negative; in fact it is one of the underlying origins of progress. In bonsai, various

Common juniper (*Juniperus communis*) grows in peaty and chalky soils. This tree has an exquisite shape, and is typical of the material that can be collected from the wild. However, at 1.5m (5ft) high this particular tree is too large to make ideal bonsai material.

This lovely juniper, with its gnarled, old wood has a rugged quality which would be impossible to achieve by human means. Collected from the wild in 1983, this tree needed very little training; the only major change was to alter its angle of growth from horizontal to vertical.

methods of shortening the very long time scales have been developed over the centuries. Although these shortcuts were not devised originally as a result of commercial pressure, nevertheless they are very important today both for the amateur enthusiast and for the commercial bonsai grower. Shortening the time scale not only improves the economics of bonsai, but makes it possible to enjoy a tree that much earlier. There is no doubt that both the amateur enthusiast and the commercial grower would like to see the end result of their efforts sooner, rather than later, and the various shortcuts developed over the years make this possible. The methods which are briefly described on the following pages are all explained in more detail in later chapters.

Large nursery trees

One way of shortening the time scales in bonsai is to adapt large nursery stock. I have made bonsai from trees which were 6-9m (20-30ft) tall, by reducing them to 60-90cm (2-3ft). In this way, you can save yourself several years of growing time, as well as taking advantage of the thick trunks which such trees will possess. A bonsai with a large trunk will, all things being equal, look much more impressive than a similar tree with a thin trunk. Deciduous nursery stock is particularly suitable for making into bonsai because they can produce new branches from very old wood, whereas evergreens are far more difficult. In later chapters illustrations show how bonsai have been created from large nursery stock using both deciduous and evergreen trees. The trees concerned are ordinary commercial products available from any nursery.

This nursery yew tree is ideal for converting into bonsai – it is approximately 30 years old, and 2m (6ft) high, with a trunk diameter of about 8cm (3in).

Left The 1m (3½ft) stump is all that remains of a 7.6m (25ft) hornbeam (*Carpinus betulus*), purchased from a landscape nursery and lifted in early fall. **Above** In three to four years' time the tree should make a beautiful bonsai – its trunk is notable for its fine ridges.

Above The nursery yew opposite has been reduced to 60cm (2ft). It is important not to disturb the roots. **Left** In spring plant the yew in a large seed tray and style it.

Collected trees

Another method for reducing the time scales in bonsai is to use "collected trees". This term normally refers to trees which have been collected from the wild – mountains and forests – but I would like to think that "collecting" embraces a much wider range of source material than this. You can, for instance, collect trees from your garden, or from friends' gardens; you can also collect from hedges, old orchards, disused quarries, railway lines and slag heaps.

The great advantage of collecting is that the trees will have been growing for many years without interference from man. In addition, the elements and the passage of time will have made them into very desirable potential bonsai material. In high mountainous regions where the growing conditions are harsh, trees grow naturally stunted, and will assume interesting twisted shapes because of the effects of wind and snow. Adapting collected trees for bonsai is described in detail in Chapter Five.

Bonsai material can be found in many places; this beech tree grows in my front garden. Recognizing its potential, I cut it down to 1m (3ft) to encourage a new leader and new branches, and undercut the roots so that the tree can be lifted a year later in the spring.

Left This beautiful little common juniper was found growing in a pocket of gravel on a high mountainside. Such trees should be lifted very carefully to avoid damaging the roots. **Above** This common juniper was a tree found growing in the wild. Its long, slender shape made it an ideal subject for a literati tree, and it required virtually no styling, although the foliage needs further refinement.

Air layering

Air layering is an ancient Chinese method of propagation whereby a trunk or branch is turned into a tree within a relatively short space of time. Although air layering is successful with most types of tree, it is important to know exactly which varieties lend themselves to this technique. The table on pp 62-3 gives a list of suitable species and indicates the time it takes for them to root.

Air layering is a very simple process. Basically, it consists of removing the bark around the branch, or portion of trunk, which is to be air layered. There are numerous variations on the amount of bark removed; alternatively, you can use a tourniquet. The peeled area is then covered with a ball of sphagnum moss, and wrapped in a piece of clear, or black, polythene. In a very short space of time (generally anything from six weeks to a year) roots will appear from the portion of branch just above where the cut has been made (or the tourniquet applied), forming a new tree which can then be used for bonsai.

There are several reasons for air layering trees. The first is aesthetic: you can select almost any portion of a trunk or a branch which has an attractive shape, and thus has the potential for being made into a good bonsai (ie the shape of the branch alone resembles a perfect tree), layer it and, in next to no time, you will have a finished tree. The second reason is economic: air layerings are virtually free. A tall nursery tree can be layered progressively from the top downward, producing a number of trees in a short period of time. The tree shown on pp 56-7, for example, produced as many as ten or eleven layerings in the course of one growing season. The various refinements of the air layering process are described on pages 52-63.

Simulating age

The fact that bonsai is essentially an illusion makes the task of creating the impression of age that much easier.

By using shortcuts or by applying cosmetic devices, a young tree can be made to look much older than it really is. There are specific visual characteristics which immediately create an impression of age: a gnarled trunk with rough bark; branches which hang downward instead of springing upward as is the case with young trees; roots which radiate uniformly from the trunk and then

This Chinese juniper, trained in the formal upright style, was produced from air layering two years ago. It is now over 60cm (2ft) tall, and has a trunk 25mm (1in) thick.

merge gradually into the soil, giving an impression of immense stability, and bringing to mind the image of a tree which, despite years of soil erosion, still stands firm; a tapered trunk and fine branches which are normally seen only in mature specimen trees.

An expert bonsai grower is able to create all these effects, but in such a way that the uninitiated viewer would never guess that the tree has been aged artificially. Some may regard such methods as cheating, but in my view, as long as the results are acceptable, the means are unimportant.

As you become more proficient in bonsai, you will undoubtedly want to experiment with different trees and different techniques, and you will also want to see the results fairly quickly. The techniques described in this chapter will enable you to achieve these aims. Many have been used for generations, while others are still being developed. The reader should find learning the theory and practice of these techniques both fascinating and rewarding.

It should now be obvious that growing bonsai from seed is not the only way of creating these trees, and also that you do not need to wait half a lifetime before you have an attractive bonsai tree.

Interrupt the flow of sap by cutting away a ring of bark, or by applying a tourniquet. Wrap moistened moss around the cut, or tourniquet, and cover with clear plastic.

This zelkova was air layered toward the end of the growing season, which meant that there was insufficient time to produce roots; they will appear next growing season.

4 Air layering

The Chinese have long been noted for their ingenuity: the wheel, the magnetic compass, high-fired ceramics, gunpowder, and indeed bonsai, are just some of the inventions attributed to them. The propagation of plants by means of air layering is yet another useful invention which is believed to be of Chinese origin.

Air layering has probably been practiced for the last 1500 years and is still widely used to this very day. The ancient Chinese might have discovered the process purely by chance: for example, by noticing a tree or branch which had partially snapped and then rooted itself in the ground.

In the hot and humid conditions of the tropics, air layering is a quick, and therefore frequent, process; in India, for instance, many varieties of fruit tree, such as mango and guava, are propagated by air layerings. The usual method is to wrap a lump of wet clay around a partially severed branch. The ball of clay is then tied on with burlap sacking, and in a matter of weeks a mass of roots will have formed.

The main advantage of air layering is that it results in a mature tree, which can produce fruit from an early age, in a very short space of time. This, of course, makes it an ideal method for bonsai, as it enables you to produce a mature tree in a fraction of the time it takes to grow a tree of similar trunk thickness from seed or a cutting. In addition, it enables you to select a branch which has the most desirable shape and character.

It would seem surprising, therefore, that despite its many attractions, air layering is not used today as a commercially viable method of bonsai production. The reason usually given by nurseries is that air layering is too labor-intensive. However, I suspect that the real reason is that one would soon run out of stock, or parent plant material,

Wisteria, with its fragrant blossoms, makes an attractive flowering bonsai. This Japanese woodcut print by Hiroshige III is entitled "Wisteria and Swallows" and is part of my Japanese picture collection.

A Deshojo mountain maple grown in the twin trunk style. Although admired mainly for its carmine leaves, the tree is also very beautiful without its foliage, especially in late fall when the twigs are still an iridescent red.

if all the choicest branches were used for air layerings. As in the case of material collected from the wild, the supply is to a large extent limited and, once exhausted, it will be a long time before more material of the same quality is available.

Where the amateur bonsai enthusiast is concerned, however, air layering is an ideal method of propagation as it is simple, cheap and quick. Those who have tried it will, I am sure, agree that it is extremely satisfying to see roots emerge from almost nothing in a matter of weeks. In fact, air layering is one of the most exciting processes in gardening.

Air layering considerably reduces the time needed to produce a bonsai. It would take up to ten years before wisteria grown from seed flowered, whereas an air-layer wisteria will flower next season. A single plant can provide several air layerings. In this case, the parent plant has been divided in two: the 15-20cm (6-8in) base (above), and the top (right).

Basic principles

The technique of air layering is based on deliberately interrupting the flow of sap to a branch. When this happens, the branch will fight to survive; either by bridging the restriction, or by sending out new roots to draw moisture and nutrients from its immediate environment.

In essence, there are two basic methods of interrupting the flow of sap to the branch; however, there are also many variations on these. In the first method you cut a ring of bark from around the branch or trunk, while in the second you apply a tourniquet around the branch so that sap cannot flow through the bark. Because the process of interrupting the sap flow is such a traumatic one, it is often advisable to leave a tiny sliver of bark to act as a bridge, or feeder, so that the end of the branch will continue to obtain nourishment, albeit at a much slower rate.

Matching method to tree

Your choice of a suitable method of air layering will depend largely on the variety of tree: for example, some varieties respond well to complete removal of a ring of bark from the branch, while others may find the shock too great and will die as a result.

With experience and by experimentation, you will soon discover which variety of tree responds best to any particular method. However, I find that complete bark removal is most successful with the following varieties: Japanese maple, trident maple, Chinese elm, zelkova, all the junipers, willows, and cotoneaster. I have also found that, although you can take air layerings from almost any part of the tree, the best position is just below a fork of a branch. This is, in fact, the position which is

White tape marks suitable air layering points on this ten-year-old zelkova, which is approximately 2.5 m (8ft) high. Five or six trees can be created in this way.

recommended by both the Chinese and Japanese.

Air layering is particularly suited to very tall nursery trees which are usually grown as standards. These are trees which have had all their shoots removed up to a height of 1.8m (6ft), leaving a "head" of branches growing from a long stem. A typical 1.8m (6ft) tree could produce as many as nine or ten trees from just one stock plant by air layering it from top to bottom. By selecting the varieties of tree which air layer easily, and by air layering a couple of sections at a time you can produce as many as six or seven all in the space of one growing season.

MULTIPLE AIR LAYERING

It is often possible to create more than one bonsai from a single tree by using air layering. This particular 2.5m (8ft) maple was the source of no less than nine bonsai. When assessing a tree for potential air layerings, it is important to keep an open mind, and to examine all the possibilities.

The ring-bark method involves removing a ring of bark from the trunk or branch. Using a sharp scalpel, or craft knife make two cuts and peel away the bark. The width of the ring should be at least as thick as the branch or trunk, but not more than twice the thickness.

The staggered ring is a variant of the ring-bark method. Cut two half rings, staggering them so that there is a quarter, or half the width of the branch, or trunk between the two. The best position is just below a fork. This method is slower, but safer than ring-barking.

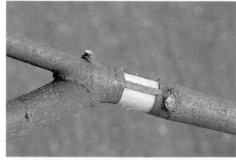

Above Multiple bridge style involves removing several slivers of bark 3mm (⅛in) wide in a ring around the branch, or trunk. **Above right** In the sliver technique a tiny sliver of bark is left as a bridge for supplying nutrients. **Below right** The wire tourniquet method is less drastic than ring-barking. Select a branch for air layering, and make a double loop of copper wire around the trunk just below the junction of the branch. Using a pair of pliers, tighten the ends until the wire cuts into the bark. Wrap sphagnum moss around the trunk, and tie plastic sheeting around it. Roots should appear in one to two years.

If skirt-style air layering is done in early summer, it will only take four to six weeks to produce a new tree. The first step is to make one circular cut, and then carefully peel the bark upward. Cut this loose bark into a number of slivers.

The second step in skirt-style air layering is to push a metal ring under the slivers of bark. This will prevent them from growing back on to the trunk.

Deciduous and evergreen trees

As a general rule, deciduous trees respond best to air layering methods which involve the complete removal of bark, while evergreen conifers respond better to either the bridge method, or the wire tourniquet method. The only exception to this rule is the juniper. Almost all the junipers layer very readily when the complete ring-bark technique is used.

The amount of time between starting the air layering and the appearance of roots varies according to the species of tree. Junipers have been known to produce roots in as little as two weeks; pines, on the other hand, are notoriously slow. White pines can take one, or even two, years to send out roots which will adequately sustain the new tree.

With pines, the wire tourniquet method is probably best, as the complete ring bark method is too drastic. You can also use the sliver variant of the ring bark method, or the multiple bridge method.

You can make air layerings from quite thick trunks and branches of the more vigorous deciduous varieties. I have, for example, successfully air layered branches and trunks from zelkova trees as thick as 10-13cm (4-5in) in diameter, and weeping willow trunks which are 15-18cm (6-7in) thick.

This cedar of Lebanon was air layered two years ago and is now 40cm (16in). The roots only appeared on one side, making the tree unstable. Score the rootless side with a scalpel, apply rooting powder and cover with moss.

Successful air layering

Air layerings are best taken in the early part of the growing season (i.e. early spring), when the sap is beginning to rise strongly. The other advantage of starting early is that you can air layer continuously from a single tree from early spring to early fall.

Some practitioners recommend wrapping the ball of sphagnum moss with clear plastic, followed by a further layer of black plastic sheeting (see p50). However, in my experience, the black plastic is unnecessary as the sphagnum moss itself will exclude much of the light from around the area of trunk or branch that is being air layered. The advantage of only using clear plastic is that you will be able to see the roots once they have formed and come through the sphagnum moss. You will, therefore, know precisely when the branch can be cut off.

The point at which the branch is severed from the parent tree is absolutely critical for successful air layerings. If it is cut off too soon, the air layering will not survive. The branch being air layered should only be cut off when sufficient root has filled the ball of sphagnum moss. This should be obvious since the root ball will be a mass of fleshy white roots. The more roots there are in the root ball, the greater the chance of the air layering's survival.

When you sever the branch, cut it cleanly. Be careful not to handle the root ball too much. Some recommend sawing half way through so that the air layering can be removed in stages. However, I have not

The essential tools and materials for making air layerings. (Clockwise from bottom left) Sharp shears for scraping away bark, Vitamin B1 solution to encourage root production, string, sphagnum moss, and some sheets of clear plastic.

The long stems of Chinese junipers make them particularly good subjects for air layering. The results can be used for groups, or for formal upright trees.

Ring-barking is the best method for air layering juniper. Cut a strip that is twice the diameter of the branch or trunk: for example, a 38mm (1½in) strip on a 19mm (¾in) trunk.

Above Dust the cuts with hormone powder, or soak moss overnight in Vitamin B1, squeeze it until just damp and wrap it around the cut. Cover the moss in clear plastic. The Vitamin B1 is not essential, but will speed up the rooting process.
Left Tie string or wire around the plastic to prevent the moisture from evaporating. Do not open until roots come through the moss. Depending on the species, roots can appear within a month, or in more difficult varieties, up to two years later. In general, deciduous trees root more quickly than evergreens.

found this to be necessary. As long as the air layering has good roots, it will survive if you cut it off immediately.

Place the sphagnum root ball in a sturdy flowerpot and fill it with pure peat. From experience, I have found that if moss peat is used instead of potting compost or sharp sand, the roots are less apt to break, and that the air layerings therefore have a much greater chance of survival. If a heavy compost, sharp sand, or grit is used its weight will compress, and thus almost certainly damage the brittle roots.

If there are a large number of leaves or branches on the newly-rooted air layering, you should remove some of them in order to reduce transpiration until the air layering is properly established. It is also advisable to stand the newly-potted air layering in a shallow saucer of water so that it can take up adequate moisture during this period. Feeding Vitamin B1 liquid will help to establish the tree quickly, but do not fertilize at this stage as it could damage the very young roots.

Ideally, freshly potted up air layerings

TABLE OF VARIETIES WHICH AIR LAYER EASILY

Common name	Botanical name	Best time to commence layering	Time taken to root	Recommended method
Broad leaved trees				
Alder	*Alnus* spp.	early summer	6 weeks	ring-bark
Beech	*Fagus* spp.	early summer	3 months	ring-bark/ tourniquet
Box	*Buxus* spp.	late spring	3 months	sliver or tourniquet
Elm	*Ulmus* spp.	early summer	6 weeks	ring-bark
Hornbeam	*Carpinus* spp.	early summer	4-5 months	ring-bark or bridge
Ivy	*Hedera* spp.	early spring	2-3 months	ring-bark
Japanese or mountain maple	*Acer palmatum A. japonicum*	early summer	6-8 weeks	ring-bark
Trident maple	*A. buergerianum*	early summer	2-3 months	ring-bark or sliver
Willow	*Salix* spp.	early summer to early fall	4-6 weeks	ring-bark
Zelkova	*Zelkova* spp.	early summer	6-8 weeks	ring-bark
Flowering and fruiting trees				
Azalea	*Rhododendron* spp.	early spring	3-4 months	bridge/tourniquet
Camellia	*Camellia* spp.	early spring	3-4 months	bridge/tourniquet
Pea tree	*Caragana* spp.	early summer	2-3 months	ring-bark
Cotoneaster	*Cotoneaster* spp.	early summer	2-3 months	ring-bark or sliver
Crab apple	*Malus* spp.	early summer	3-4 months or longer	tourniquet or sliver
Grape	*Vitis* spp.	early summer	2-3 months	tourniquet
Hawthorn	*Crataegus* spp.	early summer	5-6 months or longer	ring-bark
Jasmine	*Jasminum* spp.	early summer	3-4 months	ring-bark or sliver
Magnolia	*Magnolia* spp.	early summer	4-5 months	ring-bark or sliver

should be placed in a damp, humid atmosphere, such as a cool greenhouse, or under mist propagation, as this will encourage roots to form much more quickly. A severed air layering which has been potted up in pure sphagnum moss peat can fill a flowerpot with roots in as little as two to three weeks.

Do not attempt to pot up the freshly rooted air layering in a bonsai pot straight away; it is better to leave the air layering in a flowerpot for at least a year. The air layering should then be grown for a further year in a large seed tray, or in the open ground, to help harden off the roots, thus enabling you to manipulate and plant it in a proper bonsai pot.

In the second year after the air layering has been struck, you can begin to turn it into an attractive bonsai. Once the tree has been potted up, you can train and refine the branches and the overall structure. In time, it will be almost impossible to tell whether the bonsai has been produced from an air layering, or by one of the other more traditional methods, such as from seed, cutting, or grafting (not described in this book).

Peach	*Prunus persica*	early summer	4-6 months	ring-bark or tourniquet
Pear	*Pyrus* spp.	early summer	4-6 months	ring-bark or tourniquet
Pomegranate	*Punica* spp.	early spring	2-3 months	ring-bark or tourniquet
Cinquefoil	*Potentilla* spp.	early summer	2-3 months	ring-bark or tourniquet
Quince	*Chaenomeles* spp. & *Cydonia* spp.	early summer	3-4 months	ring-bark
Spindle tree	*Euonymus* spp.	early spring	5-6 months	sliver or tourniquet
Viburnum	*Viburnum* spp.	early summer	2-3 months	sliver or tourniquet
Wisteria	*Wisteria* spp.	early summer	4-6 weeks	ring-bark

Coniferous trees

Cedar	*Cedrus* spp.	early spring	3-4 months or longer	tourniquet
Cryptomeria	*Cryptomeria* spp.	early spring	4-6 weeks	ring-bark
False cypress	*Chamaecyparis* spp.	early spring	3-4 months	ring-bark or tourniquet
Ginkgo	*Ginkgo biloba*	early summer	3-4 months or longer	tourniquet or sliver
Juniper	*Juniperus* spp.	early spring	Chinensis var. 4-6 weeks Other var. 4-6 months	ring-bark or sliver
Larch	*Larix* spp.	early spring	2-3 months	ring-bark or tourniquet
Dawn redwood	*Metasequoia glyptostroboides*	early spring	3-4 months	ring-bark or tourniquet
Pine	*Pinus* spp. *P. sylvestris* *P. parviflora* *P. thunbergii*	early spring	6 months-2 yrs	tourniquet or sliver
Spruce	*Picea* spp.	early spring	6 months or longer	tourniquet or sliver
Swamp cypress	*Taxodium distichum*	early spring	3-4 months	tourniquet or sliver

5 | *Collected* trees

It is generally acknowledged that the best bonsai are usually those which have been collected from the wild. This is because such trees have been shaped and sculpted by nature and, as a result, have qualities which cannot easily be reproduced artificially.

In China and Japan there is a long tradition of collecting trees from the wild. As recently as 40-50 years ago professional "bonsai hunters" in Japan earned their living by collecting beautiful, old specimens from difficult and inaccessible places, such as cliffs, ravines and mountain tops. Sadly, however, this breed of men no longer exists because the wild mountainous areas of Japan have been stripped bare of these beautiful, old specimen trees.

The fate of Japan's trees illustrates the importance of responsible collecting. Removing naturally stunted trees from their native environment can become a form of ecological vandalism. The increasing awareness of the need for conservation has led many countries to introduce laws which forbid the removal of rare plants and trees growing in protected areas, or the export of rare specimens. Although bonsai do not fall into this category, trees which are obviously very old should not be taken from their native environment unless they are threatened with destruction by road works, or other man-made developments.

There are three circumstances in which collecting from the wild can be justified. Firstly, if collectable material is found growing on private land, and you are able to persuade the landowner to give you permission to remove the tree, no ethical problems arise.

Secondly, as mentioned earlier, when land is being cleared for a highway, or some other construction project. On several occasions I have come across huge tracts of forest which have been

To the inexperienced eye, this might not look like a very promising site for potential bonsai, but in fact it is typical collecting countryside. The most likely varieties would be common juniper, pines and larches. Trees of almost any size can be considered; they do not have to be large. The smaller common junipers, in particular, tend to have interesting, twisted trunks, and will make delightful little bonsai.

Mature trees, such as this Chinese juniper which is well over a hundred years old, are invariably collected trees. Imported from Japan in the 1960s, this tree is now 70cm (28in) tall with a trunk diameter of 13cm (5in). It is notable for its lovely silhouette and large area of driftwood.

razed to the ground for motorway construction, thus destroying thousands of potential bonsai.

The draining of swamps and bogs is another rich source of potential bonsai material. Such areas are commonly referred to as marginal or sub-marginal land, meaning that the soil and growing conditions are usually very poor.

However, it is just such growing conditions which produce the stunted trees which are ideal for bonsai. Trees growing on marginal land have little or no chance of survival in the longer term, which means that collecting them is quite justified.

Collecting trees from the wild should not be regarded as simply a cheap way of creating good bonsai. Although this can be true, it should not be your primary reason for collecting. The main objective should be to acquire beautiful old specimens, which could not be obtained in any other way.

Where collecting from the wild is still possible, it can of course be great fun. Nothing could be more enjoyable than going on a collecting expedition with a bonsai club, or with a few friends who are bonsai enthusiasts. The thrill and excitement of finding a beautiful specimen tree after walking for miles is a truly memorable experience. I shall never forget the ecstasy I felt on seeing acres of stunted juniper on a bleak mountainside. Fortunately, the collecting site was part of a huge private estate, and the owner was sympathetic to bonsai hunters. However, I exercised great restraint and restricted myself to taking only a few choice trees.

Alternative sites

While it may be idyllic to collect trees from traditional sites such as mountains and cliff tops, it is also becoming increasingly difficult as more mountain

Trees with bonsai potential can be found in all kinds of places – from the exotic to the garden next door. **Left** This crab apple grew too large for a nearby rockery and was about to be cut down. Although it had too many forks to be ideal bonsai material, the beautiful trunk made it worth saving.

and forest areas are set aside for conservation or recreation. Fortunately, there are alternatives. Collectable trees can be found in all sorts of surprising places, such as slag heaps, disused railway lines, old quarries and abandoned orchards.

Trees from such unlikely places not only equal those from the traditional haunts of the collector in terms of quality, but are also more varied. Trees found in quarries and slag heaps usually have very shallow and compact root systems because they have been growing in porous gravel or scree. The specimens in old orchards, and near disused railway lines are invariably stunted because they have been constantly cut back over many years.

In urban areas, the gardens of old houses awaiting demolition are a rich source of potential bonsai material. In London suburbs, for instance, I have frequently come across beautiful beech, juniper and hornbeam, which have been grown as ornamental shrubs and hedging and are at least 50-60 years old. Often the owners of derelict properties are only too glad if someone offers to take away their old, unwanted shrubs.

Left I used a chainsaw to reduce the tree to a stump about 1.2m (4ft) high. **Above** The next step was to create a new leader. **Right** Planting in an open seed bed, with a large amount of sand mixed into the soil will induce fine roots, thus allowing for removal of the old roots in about three years' time.

When to collect

As a general rule, the best time for collecting is between fall and late spring. Evergreen conifers such as pines and junipers tend to be more successful if taken during the early fall. Deciduous species, on the other hand, can be taken at any time during the dormant season, i.e. between early fall to early spring.

It is best not to collect material when the weather is very cold as the collected trees are unlikely to survive the shock, and the chances of damaging the tender roots are much greater.

However, there are occasions when rules can be broken. For instance, I have taken a tree during the height of summer (which normally would be absolutely taboo) when I felt there was no alternative. In one case, part of a forest was being dug up to accommodate a road-widening scheme. The trees I rescued were not very big – none had a trunk diameter of more than 8cm (3in), but at least half of them survived.

The survival of collected trees depends largely on the conditions in which they have been growing. Trees which grow in swampy or boggy conditions can be taken at any time of the year. Many pines, junipers and larches grow in peat bogs and, in addition, usually have very compact root systems. As a result, they are easily lifted out of the ground. Trees which grow in pockets of gravel, or in screes on the mountainside are also easy to lift for similar reasons, and can usually be taken with their root ball intact at any time of the year.

Selecting trees

It cannot be emphasized too strongly that one should always be highly discriminating in what one collects. Most novices tend to be too greedy and start collecting everything in sight. Such behavior verges on vandalism and results in trees of indifferent quality. The whole point of collecting is to find really outstanding material – material which cannot be obtained in garden centers and nurseries.

When collecting, therefore, the most essential quality of a potential bonsai is character. As far as size is concerned, there is no hard and fast rule. Those who prefer large trees will collect larger trees, while those who prefer smaller trees will obviously select their material accordingly.

Whatever the size of the tree, it is the trunk which will determine the design of a bonsai. Surprisingly large trees can be taken, provided the tops are cut down to the appropriate height. In the case of smaller trees, you should look for trees with trunks which are gnarled, or beautifully shaped, or which give the impression of age.

Tools

When out on a tree collecting expedition, your choice of equipment is usually limited by the amount you can carry. The essential tools are: a good digging spade, a sharp saw, a pair of sharp shears, some plastic bags, string, and large quantities of sphagnum moss. Although you may find sufficient moss at the collecting site, it is always safer to take some with you.

One of the secrets of success with collected material lies in the rapidity with which it can be planted. This means that for most collecting trips it is essential to have some kind of transport. A four-wheel drive vehicle is an obvious advantage if you are exploring difficult terrain; getting close to the collecting site will save you carrying a heavy tree several miles to your car.

Left This white larch was collected in 1972. It was growing out of a piece of limestone rock, which had to be removed with the tree. As with most collected trees, it cannot be conveniently classified into a recognized style, but is a mixture of informal upright and root with rock. **Above** The tree is now 74cm (29in) high, and is well established. The branches selected when the tree was first collected have been progressively refined; the pads have been encouraged to grow by constant pinching and nipping of the new growth. Every three to four years the spaces between the branches are thinned, and the roots are trimmed back so that the root ball is 25mm (1in) smaller than the new pot, and fresh soil is added.

Removing the tree

When collecting a tree, it is absolutely vital to take as much root as possible. If the tree has very few fibrous roots, it is preferable to dig a trench around the trunk and then wait another year for the fibrous roots to develop. This will ensure that the tree has a much better chance of survival when it is lifted. If this is not possible for any reason, then you will just have to hope for the best.

If the tree is too tall, you should remove as much of the unwanted growth as possible before digging it up. However, first examine the tree carefully to make sure that the branches you are about to discard can play no part in the eventual design of the bonsai. A branch that seems to be useless at first glance may, after closer inspection, be suitable for jins (driftwood) or for some other interesting design feature.

Always try to keep as much of the original soil as possible. When a tree has been lifted, wrap the root ball in burlap or plastic sheeting so that there is no loss of moisture from the roots.

A newly dug-up tree will not be able to supply its leaves with sufficient moisture to compensate for the moisture lost during transplantation. It is vital, therefore, to reduce the amount of foliage on the tree, particularly if a deciduous tree is lifted when it is in full leaf. In fact, if deciduous trees are lifted outside the dormant season, it is better to remove all the leaves.

With evergreen trees it is important not to remove too much greenery; complete defoliation of a branch will cause it to die. Unlike deciduous trees, evergreens do not produce leaves readily from defoliated branches; some leaves must be left at the tips of branches to act as sap drawers.

Aftercare

The immediate aftercare is probably the most important factor in the survival of the collected material. The interval between collecting and planting the material should be as short as possible. Obviously, the longer the tree is out of the ground the more susceptible it is to drying out. Immediately on arrival at home, it is advisable to plant the tree in a collecting bed in your garden.

A collecting pit should be about 1.2 x 1.2m (4 x 4ft) and up to 46cm (18in) deep. The pit should be filled with sharp sand or grit and must have good drainage. An alternative to a pit is a large box filled with sharp sand, or a mixture of sharp sand and peat. By planting a newly-collected tree in these conditions you will encourage it to develop a good, fibrous root system.

Some collectors advocate the use of Vitamin B1 liquid to help the trees to overcome the shock of transplantation. Many believe that Vitamin B1 liquid has almost magical powers, and thus use it extensively on collected materials. You may dip the roots in a solution containing Vitamin B1, or use it to water the whole tree. Vitamin B1 cannot do any harm – it can only do good.

Once planted the tree should ideally be kept in a closed environment. If the tree is planted in a collecting bed, it can be covered with a plastic bag. If you have used a box then a cool greenhouse is a suitable alternative. The greenhouse must be adequately shaded in summer so that it does not become too warm. The aim in both cases is to provide a very

I found this alder growing on the edge of a nearby lake. The tree was almost entirely in the water, which meant that I simply lifted it out, complete with root ball. When a tree has a large number of fine roots it can be planted directly into a training pot, or a proper bonsai pot. This alder only requires a minimum amount of basic trimming and, within a year, it should make quite an acceptable bonsai. Alders thrive in water and will benefit from being stood in a basin of water throughout the growing season. These trees are vigorous growers and will need to be repotted each year.

This larch was collected from a peat bog in Scotland during the very hot, dry summer of 1976. The top of the tree had died and only one side branch was still alive. **Below** It was planted in a large pot and the dead leader was shortened. Over the next two years most of the remaining live branches were removed or jinned, leaving only one main branch sweeping to the left. **Left** The tree is now 74cm (29in) high, with a trunk diameter of 10cm (4in).

humid atmosphere so that transpiration is reduced, thus alleviating the strain on the root system and helping the tree to recover as quickly as possible.

It is inadvisable to feed a newly-collected tree unless it is growing very vigorously, as can sometimes be the case if the tree has been lifted with a large number of roots. If a tree is obviously struggling to survive, do not feed it under any circumstances. Overeager and premature feeding can do more harm than good. If you follow these guidelines, you should find that the majority of the trees you collected from the wild, or from alternative sites, will not only survive, but will start to thrive.

Toward the end of 1986, the tall, jinned leader was carved out with a router, and the base of the trunk was partially hollowed out. This was done to create the impression of a rugged, wind-battered tree which has survived the elements for many, many years.

71

Potential bonsai can be found in all kinds of seemingly unlikely places. **Above** This example of Chinese privet was collected from the local garbage dump. Initial trimming and training only took a few minutes, which proves that it does not necessarily take years to grow a bonsai. **Right** Hedging plants, such as Chinese privet, make particularly good subjects for bonsai as they are vigorous plants which are used to growing in harsh conditions. This specimen is now well on its way to being an attractive bonsai.

A Scots pine (*Pinus sylvestris*) which was collected 15 years ago as a young sapling, and is being trained in the cascade style. Although the trunk and foliage have developed considerably over the years, the tree still needs refining. In the spring, it will be replanted in a tall cascade pot and the foliage will be thinned into pads.

Training the tree

Once a collected tree is growing healthily, the next step is to train it into a fine bonsai. However, do not be too impatient to start training new trees. Japanese collectors always leave a tree to grow for at least a couple of years before beginning any training. While it may not be necessary to wait that long, you must be sure that the tree is growing vigorously.

Always take your time about deciding on the design of a tree. Impatience, or an unsuitable design may ruin a potentially beautiful tree. With most collected trees, much of the design work has already been done by nature and the bonsai

artist's role is merely to enhance their beautiful qualities to the full. If in doubt, always seek another informed opinion or, if possible, consult a bonsai master who may be able to suggest ways in which the tree can be better designed.

The design features of collected trees should never be overdone, or the natural character of the collected tree will be lost. Because collected trees have been shaped by nature, they seldom fall into any conventional bonsai style. You should not feel disappointed by this. Indeed, it would be a mistake to force the tree to conform to a recognized formal style. The freshness and vitality of an informal design far outweighs the convenience of being able to classify it.

Incorporating driftwood into a bonsai design produces a dramatic effect. Usually, driftwood is created by stripping bark from a live tree, or by using a tree that is already partly dead. However, the method illustrated here which involves wrapping a living tree around a dead host tree produces natural driftwood more quickly than other methods. **Right** Junipers make good host trees as their wood is long-lasting and does not rot easily. **Far right** This four-year-old juniper was developed from a cutting and now has a trunk about 13mm (½in) thick.

Above To prepare the living tree, completely remove the bark from one side. Placing the stripped side against the host tree, tie the two tightly together. You can use fine copper or brass nails to pin the living tree to the dead host tree, and soft plastic string to help with support.
Left The tree is wrapped tightly around the host tree. It should now be planted in a pot, or in the open ground, and left to develop. The trunk will gradually thicken, expanding and filling any crevices in the host tree. Over a period of four to five years, the live tree will callous and adhere to the host tree, until the viewer will be unable to tell that the bonsai was formed from two separate trees.

6 Bonsai from nursery stock

A view of the pine beds at the bonsai nursery run by my wife Dawn. These pines have been individually selected from commercial nurseries for their potential as bonsai, and they will all be trained in due course.

It never occurs to most beginners that it is possible to use nursery stock as raw material for bonsai. And yet, if a bonsai is well-designed, few people would ever suspect that it had been created from ordinary nursery or garden center material. Despite its enormous potential, however, this source of bonsai is seldom tapped to its full extent. This is partly due to ignorance, and partly because of snobbery. There are bonsai collectors who would never consider using ordinary nursery stock, regarding it as second-rate. However, this attitude is changing gradually, and as more and more people become interested in the creative side of bonsai, greater use will be made of nursery material.

The term "nursery stock" is used to describe those trees and shrubs which are sold at retail gardening outlets, such as garden centers and nurseries. Nursery trees are available in all shapes and sizes, but for commercial reasons they are mostly on the small side. The trees are usually sold in 1-3l (5-9in) containers, and are up to 1.2m (4ft) tall. There are exceptions of course, and you can sometimes find trees as high as 4.5m (15ft), growing in 25-30l (12-15in) pots, or containers.

The greatest advantage of using nursery stock for bonsai is the extremely wide choice of species, shapes and sizes on offer. This variety is particularly valuable if you intend to create larger bonsai. Although it may be possible to collect suitable trees from the wild, they tend to be ordinary forest species such as pines, larches, beech, oak and juniper. In the Western hemisphere, it is almost imposssible to find ornamental species, such as Japanese maple, berberis and other exotics outside garden centers. Ironically, however, the best specimens in garden centers do not make ideal material for bonsai. Instead, you should look for the "seconds" or

Fifteen years ago this specimen Japanese mountain maple was 38cm (15in) high with a trunk diameter of less than 25mm (1in); it is now 76cm (30in) high with a trunk diameter of 8cm (3in). The fine ramification of the branches has been developed by constant pinching of the growing tips. Maples are best viewed in winter, as it is only then that the structure and tracery of the branches can be fully appreciated.

rejects, which tend to have crooked trunks, distorted branches and sparse foliage. Such specimens will make extremely interesting bonsai because the trunks and branches will adapt fairly easily to being shaped.

Another reason why nursery trees make such good raw material for bonsai is that most of them are sold in containers. Container-grown material offers enormous possibilities because it can be worked on at almost any time of the year. In addition, the root system will almost certainly be very compact, allowing you to repot them into a bonsai pot almost immediately. However, container-grown trees also suffer from the disadvantage of entangled roots; they may even have girdling roots, which go round and round the trunk base. Not only is this condition unattractive, but it may eventually choke the tree to death. This means that you should examine the roots carefully before selecting a tree.

Selecting suitable trees

You will need to develop a keen eye for potential bonsai when rummaging around in nurseries. Not only is the choice bewildering, but often the trees which are most interesting to a bonsai enthusiast are those which are kept at the back of the sales area as being of least interest to the ordinary customer.

Most nursery trees can be converted quite easily into acceptable bonsai, provided you are prepared to be fairly ruthless in the initial pruning of the top growth and roots. Nursery trees are grown primarily for their healthy foliage, which means that they tend to be top-heavy for bonsai purposes, and that the trunks are relatively thin in comparison to the branches. It is important, therefore, to choose a tree with a trunk that has a fairly thick base, and branches which start quite low down

on the trunk; trees with thin trunks and very leggy branches are of limited potential.

When selecting a tree, there are various points you should consider. The first criterion is the trunk. Faced with a bewildering array of trees, the natural tendency is to look for those with the thickest trunks. However, the shape and taper of the trunk are as important as the overall thickness: it should be broad at the base and taper gradually all the way to the top.

Next, you should examine the roots. Nursery trees are often planted by automatic potting machines, which means that the roots are not given the opportunity to spread out properly. In addition, the trees are usually planted a couple of inches deeper than necessary, therefore there will invariably be one or two inches of trunk below the soil surface. By feeling around the base of the trunk just below the soil level, you should be able to get some indication of the structure and direction of the roots.

Thirdly, you should examine the branch structure. The more branches the tree has the better, and they should spread out from the lower part of the trunk. Most of the branches should, as far as possible, be of uniform thickness; those which are either too thick or too thin should be discarded. If branches are too thick in proportion to the trunk the tree will look unbalanced; on the other hand, if the branches are too thin, they will take a long time to develop to a stage where they can be used in the ultimate design of the tree.

The condition of the foliage is not necessarily important. Trees which have been left in their containers for a long time will lose vigor. However, they will soon recover if their roots are disentangled, they are repotted in a large container, and then given a small dose of quick-acting fertilizer.

Almost any variety of nursery tree can be used for bonsai. This dwarf Alberta spruce (*Picea Albertiana conica*) is about 25 years old, and 1m (3½ft) tall, with a trunk diameter of 5-8cm (2-3in).

Before cutting or pruning a tree, it is worth spending some time studying it in order to determine the front, and to decide which branches to retain.

Judicious cutting has transformed an ordinary nursery spruce into a bonsai. Note how branches have been selected so that they are in tiers, thus enabling the viewer to see the trunk and branch structure. Although the basic shape of the bonsai has been determined, the tree will be further refined and developed over the coming years.

JUNIPER FROM NURSERY STOCK

Center This fine Chinese juniper bonsai has been created in just five years from nursery material similar to the tree shown on the right, which is 60cm (2ft) high, with a trunk diameter of 25mm (1in). There is some confusion about the definition of "Chinese juniper" as used for bonsai. In most Japanese bonsai books the variety Chinese juniper is often described as *Juniper sargentiana* or *Juniper chinensis* var "Shimpaku". It is characterized by smooth, tight, cordlike foliage, and is almost identical to the *Juniper media Blaauws* used in this project, except that the foliage of the Blaauws variety is bluer, and requires more pinching to produce beautiful mounds of foliage.

The first step towards transforming the tree into a bonsai is to remove it from its pot in early spring. Tease out the roots with a three-prong cultivator. This will untangle them, as well enabling you to arrange them radially.

The tree should now be planted in a shallow pot so that the roots can be trained for planting in a bonsai pot. Once the tree has been planted the branches can be wired downward so that they grow out in a radial fashion, and make the tree look older. Clip the ends of all the branches in order to create foliage pads.

Above Four months after its initial trimming and training, the juniper is well on its way towards becoming an attractive bonsai, although the foliage pads are still too meager to give the impression of a mature tree. **Left** The training of this tree differs from that described, in that for the first two years it was grown in open ground. During the second year, five air layerings were taken from superfluous branches. In the third year the tree was lifted, the roots were teased out, and it was replaced in the ground. In the fourth year the tree was planted in a large plastic seed tray so that it could be shaped and groomed into a bonsai. In the fifth year, it was wired with heavy aluminium and then potted in this fine Gordon Duffett pot. Despite the heavy wiring, the tree is now in showable condition – the only further training needed is constant pinching of the foliage tips.

Designing the tree

The shape of the trunk is the key factor in the overall design of the bonsai. Although it is possible to wire and bend the trunk into any shape you desire, it is far better to keep shaping to a minimum so that the trunk looks natural. Remember that you should always work with nature rather than against it. If, for example, a nursery tree has a fairly upright trunk, it would make sense to train it into a formal upright style. The trunk of a formal upright tree must be absolutely straight. Consequently, if there is even the slightest hint of a kink in the trunk, it must be straightened out.

The position of the branches is vital: as far as possible, they must emerge from the classic positions. The first branch should be either on the left or the right, pointing slightly forward, the next branch on the opposite side should also point slightly forward (the "twenty minutes past eight" position), while the third branch should be at the back, and so on.

In most designs, except literati, the rear branches are very important as they provide perspective to the design of the tree. Remember that the eventual overall

STRUCTURING A MAPLE
Right A Japanese maple which was lifted, complete with root ball, in fall and then wrapped in burlap. It is about 90cm (3ft) high, with a trunk diameter of 25cm (1in). When trimming a deciduous tree you can remove as much as 80 per cent of the branch structure.
Far right Select a leader which will produce a good taper as it grows. Make a slanting cut and remove all of the tree above that point. Applying tree sealant to the cuts will encourage quick healing and prevent disease.

Right It is important to spend time structuring a tree, as getting it right initially will save you a great deal of unnecessary work later. **Far right** The strong points of this specimen are its abundance of roots and the beautiful root flare. In time, these attributes will contribute towards producing a well grown tree with a balanced appearance.

shape of the tree should always be triangular; also that the crown should be slightly rounded and dense. Only mature bonsai have rounded crowns; immature or newly-trained bonsai will have thin, sparse apexes. If a nursery tree trunk does not have a good taper, you need not reject it out of hand; a good taper can always be created by chopping off the existing leader at the appropriate point, and growing a new leader. Repeated cutting back of the existing leader will, in time, produce a good, even taper.

It is important to develop good, radial roots from an early age, as it is very difficult to rectify bad roots when the tree is older. If the roots which emerge from the base of the trunk are still fairly pliable, tease them out, spread them radially, and then pin them down with pieces of wire bent into the shape of a hairpin. A good system of radial roots should resemble the spokes of a wheel; in addition, they should appear to buttress the trunk as it rises out of the soil.

As mentioned earlier, the condition of the foliage is not particularly important because it can always be improved by proper feeding; it is the actual branch structure which is important. It is

The transformation of nursery trees into bonsai can be achieved in a very short period of time. **Above** This large *Picea orientalis* is 1.6m (5½ft) high. Bought from a nursery a year previously, its branches have been thinned out, the roots have been heavily pruned, and it has been potted up into a training pot. **Left** Three hours later all the extraneous branches have been removed, and those retained have been wired down. The basic structure, therefore, has been established, and over the next few years the foliage pads will be encouraged to develop. The white marker in the pot denotes the front of the tree.

MAPLES FROM SEED

Right These two Japanese maple seedlings were allowed to grow unchecked for two years. In the third year they were cut back to 20cm (8in), which encouraged vigorous growth. Now, at four years, they have reached a height of 56cm (22in), and a trunk diameter of 8mm (5/16in).

Above Maples of this size have fairly pliable trunks, which means that they can be wired into almost any shape. I have used soft 100 per cent aluminum wire on these saplings.
Right Once wired, these trees may be carefully manipulated into the desired shape. Here a gentle "S" curve is being created.

Left This maple has been grown from seed and is now eight years old. The trunk has been trained into a pleasing "S" shape, and all the branches have been pruned well back. Over the next few years the branches will be allowed to grow freely to form the basic structure of the tree. Rapid growth of the trunk and branches will be encouraged by growing the tree in a large training pot.

Above This crab apple is being developed from nursery material. It was already a fairly mature tree with a height of about 1.2m (4ft), and a trunk diameter of 5cm (2in). A new leader is being encouraged, and the branches have all been regrown over the past two years. The branches need to be rewired at this stage, otherwise they will soon become too stiff.

This lavishly-flowering rhododenron bonsai was created from ordinary nursery stock; its beautiful pink blossoms never fail to win the admiration of the public when exhibited at London's famous Chelsea Flower Show.

essential to establish the correct branch structure from the very beginning because this is what will determine the shape of the tree for the rest of its life as a bonsai. It is, therefore, worth sacrificing some time in the early stages of development in order to perfect the structure, rather than rushing the process and then having to make corrections later on.

With deciduous nursery trees, if the branches are not in the right position or are of the wrong thickness, it is worth removing all of them, so that only the basic trunk remains. In this way, when the branches regrow, you can ensure that they emerge from exactly the right points along the trunk. Beginners are often nervous about cutting a tree back too much, although this is often essential for making a tree into a bonsai.

There is, however, one fundamental rule that many beginners forget: if you remove all the foliage from an evergreen tree it will die. The only exceptions are azaleas and rhododendrons.

Maintaining the design

Once you have created the basic structure of the bonsai, the soft young growth requires constant pinching so as to maintain the overall shape of the tree. Constant pinching will also ensure that the branches divide further into more branchlets, thereby producing what is known as good "ramification". This is painstaking work and can take years to pefect. Generally, the aim is to create a tapering, arrowhead shape for your branch structure which, together with the overall triangular shape, will make a very elegant design.

Wiring will be essential since this is what gives the tree its precise shape. Most newly-created trees will require a great deal of wiring; it is very rare to come across a tree which already has the desired shape. Wires on thinner branches need only be left for one growing season, whereas wires on thicker branches and trunks should be left on for a couple of years.

Nursery trees suited to bonsai

Deciduous trees

Acer palmatum and *japonica*	*Stephanandra incisa*
Aesculus	*Tamarix*
Amelanchier	*Ulmus* (elm)
Azalea (most varieties)	*Viburnum* (especially *V. plicatum tomentosum*)
Berberis (most varieties)	*Wisteria*
Buxus (box)	
Camellia (most varieties)	
Caragana (also known as Chinese pea-tree)	**Conifers**
Carpinus (hornbeam)	*Cedrus atlantica*
Cercidiphyllum	*Cedrus deodora*
Cercis siliquastrum	*Cedrus libani*
Chaenomeles (flowering quince)	*Chamaecyparis lawsoniana* 'Elwoodii'
Cornus (most varieties)	*Chamaecyparis obtusa* 'Nana gracilis'
Corylus (nut tree)	*Chamaecyparis pisifera* 'Boulevard'
Cotinus	*Chamaecyparis pisifera filifera*
Cotoneaster (most varieties)	*Chamaecyparis pisifera plumosa*
Crataegus (hawthorn)	*Chamaecyparis pisifera squarrosa*
Eleagnus	*Chamaecyparis thyoides* 'Andalyensis'
Escallonia	*Cryptomeria japonica* (most varieties)
Euonymus (spindle tree)	*Ginkgo biloba*
Fagus (beech)	*Juniperus chinensis* (most varieties)
Forsythia	*Juniperus communis* (most varieties)
Hedera (ivy)	*Juniperus media* (including 'Blaauws')
Ilex (holly)	*Juniperus media* 'Hetzii'
Laburnum	*Juniperus media pfitzeriana*
Ligustrum (privet)	*Metasequoia*
Lonicera nitida (hedging honeysuckle)	*Picea abies* 'Echiniformis'
Magnolia (*stellata* and *liliflora* only suitable)	*Picea orientalis*
Malus (crab apple)	*Picea glauca* or 'Albertiana conica'
Morus (mulberry)	*Pinus* (most species) In particular
Nothofagus (most varieties of southern beech)	*Pinus mugo*
Potentilla	*Pinus parviflora* 'Templehof'
Prunus (most varieties except *P. laurocerasus)*	*Pinus parviflora* 'Negeshi'
Pyracantha	*Pinus strobus nana*
Quercus (oak)	*Pinus sylvestris* (most varieties, in particular 'Beuvronensis')
Rhododendron (small-leaf and small-flowered varieties only)	*Taxodium distichum*
Salix (willow)	*Taxus baccata* (English yew)
Sophora japonica	*Taxus cuspidata*

7 Bonsai from extra-large nursery stock

Large bonsai, like large paintings, have a particular quality of their own. Just as the impact of a large painting is different from that of a small one, so in bonsai, the impression created by a large bonsai is quite different from that created by a much smaller tree.

A "large" bonsai ranges from 0.6-1.2m (2-4ft) in height and may weigh as much as 50-70kg (110-154lb). Such trees convey a feeling of immense power and grandeur, and their regal appearance has prompted many bonsai collectors to concentrate almost exclusively on large specimen trees. As a result, increasing numbers of these trees are appearing at important bonsai exhibitions.

The raw material for large bonsai is less generally available than that described in the previous chapter. In the horticultural trade, such trees are known as "landscape" or "amenity" trees, and they are grown for professional landscape gardeners in specialist nurseries. Landscape nursery trees have stems which are 1.8-2.5m (6-8ft) high, with trunk diameters from 8cm (3in) upwards. Some of the very large specimens are known as "extra-heavy trees", as they can be as much as 7.6-9m (25-30ft) high, with a root ball weighing up to half a ton. Believe it or not, even these trees have potential for bonsai!

Converting such material into bonsai is not advisable for the bonsai novice as it requires experience, and the use of specialist techniques. For the more advanced enthusiast, however, large trees of this kind offer enormous possibilities for creating very spectacular bonsai.

Although this Chinese juniper has been trained and developed using all the traditional bonsai techniques, strictly speaking, at 2.5m (8ft), it is too large to be described as a bonsai. Nevertheless, trees such as this have a beauty all their own. This specimen was imported from Japan by a bonsai nursery in Holland.

Sources of large trees

There are not many nurseries which specialize in landscape material; partly because it is a very specialist market,

This winter flowering cherry (*Prunus subhirtella*) is a good example of what can be achieved by adapting a large nursery tree. The original tree was nearly 2m (7ft) high; four years ago it was reduced to 46cm (18in). Since then a new leader and all the branches have developed, the trunk is now 10cm (4in) in diameter, and the tree is 80cm (32in) high. Although the tree needs further training, it is quite an acceptable bonsai.

and partly because many of the public authorities grow their own trees. Even if you can find a nursery which produces this type of material, it will not necessarily sell to the public, although you may be able to persuade them to sell you one or two trees.

Some city corporations dig up old, unwanted, or damaged trees and, if you can persuade the authorities to let you have the trees, they could prove to be very acceptable material for bonsai. It pays, therefore, to be observant.

If all else fails, then the only choice left is to grow your own large specimen trees. This is not as difficult as is commonly imagined. All you need is some spare land and a little patience.

Growing your own trees

Most varieties of tree, if planted as pencil-thick seedlings, can increase as much as 5-8cm (2-3in) in trunk diameter over 8-10 years. Some of the more vigorous varieties, such as hornbeam and trident maple, can produce a trunk diameter of 10-13cm (4-5in) over the same period. As a general rule, the warmer the climate the more prolific and vigorous the growth.

Vigorous growth can also be promoted in various ways: feeding the tree heavily during the growing season; keeping the area around the trunk free from weeds so that the tree does not have to compete for nutrients; and encouraging shoots to develop from the base, which not only encourages the trunk to thicken, but also gives it a better taper.

In fact growing your own large specimen trees can produce results far superior to those of professional landscape nurseries because you can control the shape, and the trunk development in the initial stages. Many street trees are cultivated as "standards", which means that their basal shoots and lower branches are lopped off, leaving a clean stem. This method of growing trees does not encourage the trunk to thicken as quickly, nor does it produce a good taper.

This nursery yew is ideal bonsai material: 1.5-1.8m high, with an 8cm (3in) diameter trunk, it is about 30 years old. Regular clipping by the nursery has given it a compact, bushy appearance; in addition, its roots have been undercut, which means that it can be lifted easily from the ground and potted up. If you had collected a similar tree from your garden, or from the wild, the roots would not be as fine. This characteristic is one of the great advantages of using nursery material.

If you can afford to wait for up to two years, you should consider air layering the top of the tree. Alternatively, you can create an instant bonsai in a couple of hours by cutting off the top of the tree, and discarding it.

I decided that this particular tree would be more interesting if I created a jin (driftwood). The first step is to decide upon a suitable point for cutting the trunk.

Saw one-third to one-half way through the trunk, cutting away from the direction of the trunk, and pointing the blade up. Bend the trunk until it snaps, and wrench it off. Tearing creates a more natural texture than cutting.

The tree has been reduced to 90cm (3ft). The next stage involves unwrapping the burlap and examining the roots. Ideally, they should spread radially from the trunk.

When designing a tree one of the most vital decisions you will make concerns the selection of its front and back. The determining factors will be the position of its roots and branches.

When shaping a tree, try to keep a completely open mind, and continue to study the tree as you alter it. Halfway through the trimming, you may well decide that the tree should be approached from another angle. Here, for instance, I decided to change the back of the tree to the front, thus allowing more jin to appear in front.

In general, you create a jin by peeling back the bark to reveal dead wood. However, you can also carve into the wood with a router. This gives the trunk a more interesting appearance, and adds a new dimension to the art of creating bonsai – it becomes living sculpture.

A router is a high-speed power tool, and should be used with great care. It is essential always to hold the router firmly; if it slips, or kicks-back it could cause serious injury. **Above** Carve a small amount of wood at a time, and move slowly, otherwise you could damage, or even kill large sections of the tree. **Left** The basic structure of the bonsai is complete. In a cold climate, the tree will require winter protection – preferably in an unheated greenhouse. Yew is particularly suited to sculpting and jin, as is juniper, larch, and pine. Jins are rarely featured in the design of deciduous trees, partly because the wood of many broadleaves is not long-lasting.

Selecting suitable trees

Most of the trees you will find in specialist nurseries are standards. These are trees which have a straight stem, no branches for 1.8-2.5m (6-8ft), and a crown of branches at the top. They are normally cultivated in close proximity, which encourages them to grow straight.

Street trees are usually deciduous because they are able to withstand the polluted city air far better than their evergreen counterparts. The reason for this is that when the pores of their leaves become choked by fumes and dirt, deciduous trees are able to rejuvenate themselves by shedding their leaves each year. Evergreens, on the other hand, do not shed their leaves as often, and hence are unable to rid themselves of the dirt which collects in their pores. On the rare occasion when evergreens

TRIDENT MAPLE PROJECT
When turning a deciduous tree into a bonsai, it is important to attempt to visualize the future appearance of the tree. **Right** This trident maple has the potential to become a powerful tree with beautiful roots that appear to grip the soil. At this stage, it has been grown in the ground for eight years, and its trunk has thickened from 25mm (1in) to 15cm (6in). The tree was grown over a stone to encourage the roots to develop flare, while nipping the top has increased the number of branches near the base. **Far right** A new leader was chosen, not because it was the thickest branch, but because it grew at the desired angle.

Right Trident maples are vigorous trees, which means that these cuts will heal in a couple of years. In fact, scars such as these can make the trunk appear gnarled and old, thus adding to the attraction of the tree. **Far right** When deciding on a tree's front, you should study it from all angles. Remember that the trunk will determine the appearance of the tree. Here, the tree has been placed in an alternative position, giving the leader a gradual taper, which is more pleasing than the previous rather sudden slant.

are used as street trees, they are normally tall, straight varieties.

Landscape trees, therefore, have limited potential as bonsai, unless you can find trees with slightly flawed trunks. This means looking for trees which have twisted trunks, or trunks which have been damaged at some stage. Certain varieties of tree, such as hornbeam, have fluted trunks extending 0.9-1,2m (3-4ft) from the base which can look very impressive. (*See illustration on p101.*)

The next characteristic to look for in landscape trees is a good radial root system. The great advantage of landscape trees is that they will invariably have a very compact and fibrous root system, because they will have been undercut frequently in order to facilitate eventual lifting and transplanting. This compact root system makes them more amenable to training in pots.

A San José juniper collected from a friend's garden in 1982. It was about 1.5m (5ft) high, with dead wood at the base, and the top of the canopy was composed of a mass of stiff, heavy, tangled branches.

View a tree from a variety of angles before deciding which branches to cut; to a large extent, your choice will determine the front and back of the tree.

Tilt the tree in different directions to help you to decide on its best angle. Keep some of the old branches to show the jin. Repot in the spring at the chosen angle. The main attraction of this tree is its trunk, which is about 13cm (5in) thick. The tree still requires a considerable amount of shaping, but the basic structure has been determined.

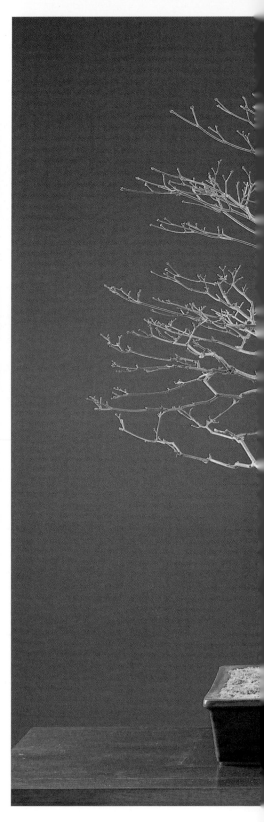

Above This San José juniper started life as an ordinary garden shrub. After about 30 years it had become too large, and was destined to be grubbed up and burnt. I rescued the tree and, under the guidance of the great bonsai Master, John Naka, turned it into a bonsai. It is now 76cm (30in) high, with a trunk diameter of 11cm (4½in). To show the tree to maximum effect, it has been planted in an exquisite Gordon Duffett container, and placed on an oak stand made from a piece of old furniture found on a garbage dump.

Above This Siberian elm (*Ulmus pumila*) was created from large nursery stock over a period of four years. The top was cut off 30cm (12in) from the base, and all the branches have been regrown. The tree is now 70cm (28in), with a trunk diameter of 10cm (4in). It is being trained in the broom style, but shaped like a typical English elm. **Left** This magnificent Japanese mountain maple is over 100 years old. The tree is so old that much of the wood has decayed, and it has to be treated regularly with wood preservative to stop further rotting.

Instead of being air layered, this 3m (10ft) Japanese gray bark elm was cut down to 46cm (18in) in the early spring, and by midsummer it had produced a mass of branches. Having decided on a broom style, the front was chosen by carefully examining its visible root structure. A "V" was cut into the top of the trunk, branches which would form the basis of the design were selected, and then the bottom branches were removed.

During the second year, secondary and tertiary branches were encouraged to grow, thus creating a canopy. The tree was planted in a training box rather than a flowerpot so that the roots would spread better. In three years' time, the tree will have become a bonsai.

Lifting landscape trees

As landscape trees are usually grown in the open ground, they are best lifted during the dormant season, or in early spring. If you have the choice, spring is preferable. With deciduous varieties you can cut the tree down to any height, as it will sprout readily from the base. However, with evergreen trees, complete removal of the branches will cause the tree to wither and die.

When the top has been cut off, immediately seal the wood in order to reduce moisture loss from the tree. This is particularly important for evergreens. I have found that grafting wax is effective for sealing evergreen cuts, while tar-based sealants are preferable for deciduous trees.

If the tap root has not already been removed, you should remove it immediately, along with any other roots which are growing straight down into the soil.

Aftercare

In my experience, trees which have been dug up from a nursery prefer to be grown on in a collecting bed of sharp sand for a complete growing season. This will encourage good root development, as well as inducing the top to regenerate.

Treat the tree almost like a giant cutting. Support the trunk with a few stout stakes. This is very important because any rocking movement will disourage roots from growing properly, which, in turn, will retard the tree's recovery considerably. If the tap root has been removed, it may not be necessary to support the trunk, as the tree will then be more stable.

During the initial part of the growing season the tree should be watered frequently, but it should not be fertilized until you are certain that it is growing well. Premature application of fertilizer will severely damage the roots.

Allow the tree to grow freely for a full year, so that it will produce a large number of new branches. It is a good idea to establish the front and back of the tree from an early stage, so that you can encourage the new leader to develop exactly where you wish it to be. Although a clearly-defined leader is not important if the tree is being developed for a broom style, it is essential for all other styles. Once the desired number of branches are growing in the correct places, they can be pinched and stopped at regular intervals in order to develop fine ramifications.

If a landscape tree has obvious potential for air layering, and if you are prepared to wait for a couple of years, then you should retain the top rather than discarding it immediately. In this way, your original tree could provide you with several extra trees for virtually nothing. (For full details on air layering techniques, see Chapter Four.)

Matching style to tree

Because of their straight trunks, landscape or amenity trees are particularly suited for developing into broom style bonsai. Varieties such as zelkova and elm lend themselves to making broom style trees and can be turned into acceptable bonsai in as little as three to four years. Varieties such as trident maple, beech and hornbeam produce new leaders very quickly (usually two to three years) and therefore can be used for the more traditional styles, such as informal upright, upright, or slanting.

The greatest advantage of using landscape trees for bonsai is, of course, their very thick trunks: not only does this shorten the time scale for producing a mature bonsai, but it enables you to create an entirely different type of bonsai from the more traditional miniature varieties. Developing bonsai from these large specimens is very satisfying, and offers a whole new range of possibilities for the true enthusiast.

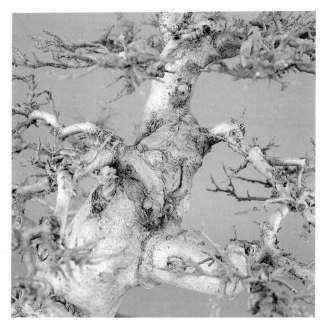

Left The superb quality of this trident maple makes it a true specimen tree. **Far left** Constant pinching and pruning of the branches has resulted in this fine ramification of the twigs.

8

Bonsai from hedges

A typical country hedge of hawthorn, which also includes a huge oak tree. The hawthorn in the foreground has a beautifully-twisted trunk about 13cm (5in) in diameter, and will make an excellent bonsai in three to four years' time, once it has been established and trained. Its roots were prepared for lifting last spring; in the coming spring the tree will be dug up, and planted in a deep collecting box.

Hedges, particularly rural hedges, are traditionally associated with the English countryside: the popular image of rural England is still one of gentle, rolling pastures, crisscrossed every so often by neatly-trimmed hedges. Yet hedges are not exclusive to Britain; they have been widely used throughout Europe for at least five centuries, and in the United States for the past 200 years. In modern times, ornamental hedges are planted extensively all over the world.

Hedges are used primarily as boundaries, thus they are by their very nature low and compact: a typical hedge is usually no more than 1.2-1.5m (4-5ft) high. Consequently the plant material most suitable for this purpose is shrubs and bushes. If trees are included in a hedge, they must be able to withstand constant pruning and cutting back.

It should be obvious to the bonsai enthusiast that a hedge contains a wealth of ready-made potential bonsai. In fact, hedging material seems to have all the basic qualities needed for bonsai. The plants, or trees, in a hedge will have been growing for many years, and during that time they will have been constantly pruned and chopped back to a reasonable size. This process thickens the trunk, produces compact bushes with interesting, twisted shapes, and means that a great deal of the basic shaping and pruning will already have been done. In addition to these qualities, hedging material invariably stands up well to pruning, and because the plants grow in such close proximity, they are accustomed to root restriction, and will tolerate shade and poor light conditions. Obviously, hedges are also a much more convenient source of bonsai than material growing in the wild. Given all these desirable qualities, it is hardly surprising that more and more bonsai enthusiasts are discovering that hedges are an extremely rich, convenient source

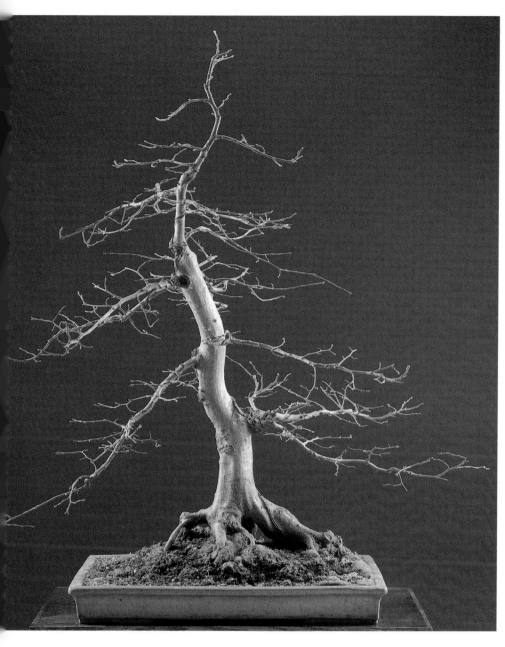

When I acquired this hornbeam (*Carpinus betulus*) it had been growing in a training box for a couple of years, the top had been removed, and there was no new leader in sight. I immediately saw its potential, and laid a wager that it could be transformed into a showable tree within two years. First, I cut off all the branches. When new shoots appeared, I selected those which I planned to develop into branches. Their tips were pinched continuously, and by the end of the first growing season many were 6mm (¼in) thick. Less than two years later the tree was shown at London's Chelsea Flower Show. Over the next few years the branch structure will be further refined, and the apex will be rounded.

of raw material for potential bonsai masterpieces.

Hedges fall into two broad categories: rural hedges; and garden hedges. The former tend to be confined to traditional varieties of tree and shrub which respond well to constant cutting back and coppicing. The table on p107 lists the species most commonly found in rural hedges, as well as some of the less popular varieties.

Suburban hedges, on the other hand, tend to be a mixture of traditional and ornamental species, such as beech, yew, hedging honeysuckle, hornbeam, hawthorn, berberis, laurel, leyland cypress, box, forsythia, holly, cotoneaster, privet and pyracantha. The list is endless; and you will recognize straightaway that almost all these plants, with the exception of laurel and leyland cypress, make excellent bonsai.

Selecting suitable Bonsai material

As in any collecting situation, not every tree within a hedge is suitable for bonsai: some may be so badly shaped that they would be of little use whatsoever; some may have indifferent trunks; others will have very poor roots, or branches. You will, therefore, have to be highly discriminating in selecting specimens.

When you look at a hedge you will notice that one or two trees tend to dominate the rest, and also that some have much thicker trunks than others. When selecting a plant, try to find one with all the qualities needed for making a bonsai: good root spread, shapely trunk, good taper, and so on. Remember that the trees with the most shapely trunks, may not necessarily be those with the thickest trunks.

If you see a tree in a hedge which has the potential for bonsai, do not rush headlong to take it out; it is worth taking the time to plan its collection very carefully. After all, the tree has taken years to grow into that marvellous shape, and it would be a great pity to spoil it all by hasty and careless digging.

Removing hedging material

If a hedge is being grubbed up, or removed because it is no longer wanted, the trees should be rescued and planted immediately. However, if this is not the case, you should not remove the plant until the dormant season, or early spring. Ideally, if there is no hurry to remove the plant, you should spread the lifting operation over a period of at least two years. This is particularly true of very old specimen trees, as their roots will almost invariably be deeply imbedded in the

HORNBEAM PROJECT
Hornbeams are one of the easiest varieties of tree to make into bonsai. This is because they produce numerous shoots in a very short space of time, which facilitates training. This massive hornbeam is 1.2m (4ft) high, with a trunk diameter of 15cm (6in). It was taken from an urban hedge three years ago as a stump with all its branches and top removed.

A new leader has been encouraged to develop, giving the tree a good taper. This is the third crop of branches; each year the previous year's shoots have been removed, with the exception of those at the top. This encouraged rapid thickening up of the new leader.

This close-up shows where a major branch was removed three years ago. The branch was growing 38cm (15in) from the base, and was cut off with a chain saw. The cut was then very roughly refined, using a power router, which is a more precise carving tool.

Right In the summer, the cut made by removing the leader was hollowed out roughly with a chain saw. **Above** Next, the cut was refined with a power router. This produces a much smoother finish than that given by a chain saw, thus encouraging better callousing.

surrounding area, as well as entangled with those of the other trees in the hedge.

It is best to start by digging a trench on both sides of the hedge about 60cm (2ft) away from the trunk of the tree you wish to remove. Any roots that you come across should be cut off with the spade, or with sharp shears. It is important to remove the tap root; this may prove to be a major operation, however, as it is bound to be well established. After cutting back the major roots, fill the trench with sharp sand to encourage the development of fine roots, and then leave the tree to grow undisturbed until the following spring.

Once you have decided to lift a tree, dig a trench around it. This should be at least 60-90cm (2-3ft) away from the trunk, the width of a spade across, and at least 30cm (1ft) deep. Once again, cut off any roots you find. Now widen the trench gradually until you are about 30-38cm (12-15in) away from the trunk base. Continue to use your spade or shears to cut off any roots which you encounter, in order to make the lifting easier. If possible, dig under the base of the tree so that the tap root, as well as any other roots that grow straight into the soil, can be severed. This may be hard work, but will be worth the effort.

If the tree has a good compact root system it will be possible to create a root ball, which can then be lifted easily out of the ground. If fibrous roots are few and far between, it is advisable to leave the tree in position for another year, so that the secondary fibrous roots can be encouraged to grow by filling up the trench with sharp sand, or gravel, and covering it with soil. In the meantime, some top pruning of the tree will encourage new branches to form lower down on the trunk.

A closer view of the new apex as seen from the front of the tree. The taper is already quite pleasing, and the cut area at the back is barely noticeable. The crown of the tree is being trained like a small bonsai; however, all the branches must be in the right positions.

A rear view, showing where the cut was made to develop a new leader. The cut is deeper than might appear to be necessary, so that when it eventually calluses over, the area will blend in with the trunk.

Aftercare

When you remove a tree, always take as much root as possible. Initially, the tree should be planted in a large bed of sharp sand (30-46cm [12-18in] deep) to encourage the growth of fine roots.

Deciduous trees can be cut to their eventual bonsai height almost immediately. Nearly all the branches can be removed, without the plant suffering; invariably new shoots and branches will appear in the following spring.

With evergreens, however, you should be careful not to remove too much foliage from the branches as this could kill the tree. The green leaves at the end of branches act as sap drawers, and thus play a crucial role in keeping the tree alive. Try to maintain an equal balance between the amount of root left on the tree, and the branches and foliage.

It is probably true to say that the success rate for bonsai created from hedging material is higher than that for material taken from the wild. This is mainly because material collected from hedges can be controlled much more carefully than that taken from the wild.

Right A front view of the hornbeam taken during the summer. When the scar in front callouses over it will blend in with the trunk. Alternatively, the scar could be further emphasized by hollowing out the trunk, thus turning the tree into a split trunk or "sabamiki" tree. **Far right** A rear view of the tree showing the prolific development of new branches. These should not be allowed to develop into final branches; they may be too thick by the time they are required. However, it is important to develop the apex and new leader.

Above top A privet stump which was taken from a hedge. It is nearly 13cm (5in) in diameter, and all the shoots have grown during the last six months. Over the next few years, a single new leader will be encouraged to develop, and the rest of the branches will be removed. In this way, the tremendous potential of the trunk can be exploited, resulting in an attractive, tapering tree. **Above** An 8cm (3in) sycamore stump which has had all the branches removed. If sycamores are kept pot-bound, their leaves decrease in size.

HEDGING MATERIAL

Hedges provide potential bonsai material in all kinds of shapes, sizes, and species. **Right** This English elm was removed from a country hedge about a year ago. It is 15cm (6in) in diameter, and was about 1.5m (5ft) tall, before being reduced to its present height of 46cm (18in). In three or four years' time the new leader should have thickened considerably, giving the bonsai a pleasing taper.

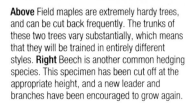

Above Field maples are extremely hardy trees, and can be cut back frequently. The trunks of these two trees vary substantially, which means that they will be trained in entirely different styles. **Right** Beech is another common hedging species. This specimen has been cut off at the appropriate height, and a new leader and branches have been encouraged to grow again.

Training into Bonsai

Almost all the varieties of tree that I have listed in this chapter will make attractive bonsai. Some respond better to heavy pruning than others, but it is worth experimenting with different species as their response will vary depending on the climate and growing conditions. In my experience beech, hornbeam, elm, ash, and hawthorn lend themselves most readily to making bonsai. Hornbeam, hedging elm, and beech are particularly easy to train as they produce numerous new branches in a very short space of time. Holly, yew, and box tend to be more difficult as they are slower growing and do not produce new shoots as readily as their deciduous counterparts. In addition, holly roots tend to be very fleshy and, when transplanted, the roots are apt to rot, while in the case of yew, the fibrous roots are difficult to establish, and therefore it is important to take as much root as possible when removing them from a hedge.

Collecting ornamental plants, such as forsythia, cotoneaster, pyracantha, and berberis is a fairly simple process, and most of the plants taken from these hedges are fairly easily adapted for making into bonsai. All these ornamentals air layer easily, which means that it is often worth the time and effort to air layer choice branches before digging up the whole tree.

Once a tree has been removed from a hedge, the process of training it into a bonsai is essentially the same as that for making bonsai from nursery stock, or from material collected from the wild. The first step is to encourage vigorous root and branch development. With deciduous species, remove all the branches except those selected for training. With evergreens, retain branches of medium thickness and discard the remainder.

Most common hedging species

Ash (*Fraxinus excelsior*)

Beech (*Fagus Sylvatica*)

Blackthorn (*Prunus spinosa*)

Elm (*Ulmus procera* and other varieties)

Field maple (*Acer campestre*)

Hawthorn (*Crataegus monogyna*)

Hazel (*Corylus avellana*)

Holly (*Ilex aquifolium*)

Hornbeam (*Carpinus betulus*)

Pedunculate oak (*Quercus robur*)

Sycamore (*Acer pseudoplatanus*)

Yew (*Taxus baccata*)

Less common species

Alder (*Alnus glutinosa*)

Apple (*Malus sylvestris*)

Briar (*Rosa arnensis*)

Broom (*Sarothamnus coparius*)

Dogwood (*Cornus*)

Elder (*Sambucus*)

Guelder rose (*Viburnum opulus*)

Lime (*Tilia cordata*)

Pine (*Pinus sylvestris*)

Poplar (*Populus*)

Privet (*Ligustrum vulgare*)

Rowan (*Sorbus aucuparia*)

Spindle (*Euonymus europaeus*)

Willow (*Salix* varieties)

Although training bonsai from hedging material may appear to be a long and tedious process, it is well worth the effort. By using this method, you will create good bonsai with impressive trunks in a relatively short space of time.

Above top When trees have been dug out of a hedge, they should be heeled immediately into the ground, or into a mound of sand. This will prevent the roots from drying out, and also protect the fine roots. Once heeled in they can be left for quite a long time before potting up. **Above left** A hornbeam collected from a local hedge which has had all the unwanted branches removed. **Above right** Hawthorn is less prolific and vigorous than hornbeam. After three years the leader is developing well, but it will take another five to seven years to become a handsome bonsai. **Left** This small English elm is only 25cm (10in) high, but it has a trunk diameter of 31cm (1¼in). It was planted in a seed tray a year ago, and is being trained as a bonsai.

9

Forest and group plantings

Most people who encounter bonsai for the first time find forest and group plantings the most appealing. The reason for this is that a successful forest planting is one of the high points of miniaturization: it can look so realistic that the viewer almost expects to hear birds singing in the trees. Man's early association with primeval forests is probably another reason why forest plantings evoke more intensity of feeling in the onlooker than a single tree.

In many respects, a group planting is one of the most difficult aspects of bonsai because it requires maximum use of aesthetic, design and horticultural principles; the bonsai artist is called upon to exercise his or her imagination and skill to the utmost. The satisfaction derived from creating a successful group planting is similar to that experienced by a landscape artist who captures a beautiful piece of scenery on a canvas. It is surprising, therefore, that despite the beauty of group plantings, not many bonsai enthusiasts devote much time or effort to their creation.

Group and forest plantings could almost be the subject of a separate book; thus, in this chapter, I have restricted myself to outlining the basic principles and techniques. This will give you enough information to become fairly proficient at making groups; however, practice makes perfect, and it is only by experimenting that you will gradually improve your skills.

Views such as this provide bonsai artists with the inspiration for forest and group plantings. Just as a painter might attempt to capture a beautiful landscape on canvas, a bonsai artist might try to recreate this scene on a miniature scale, using live trees.

What is a group?

Any composition of two or more trees constitutes a group. Groups are nearly always planted in odd numbers, partly because of tradition and partly because asymmetrical balance is more easily achieved with an odd number of trees. The generally accepted numbers are 2, 3, 5, 7, 9, 11, 13, and so on. However, if

This beautiful Chinese juniper group was created by the celebrated bonsai master John Yoshio Naka in 1984. The group consists of 19 trees aged between 10 and 25 years old; the tallest is 100cm (40in) high. The composition has immense depth and perspective, which is largely created by placing the tallest trees in the front and the smallest ones at the back. Note that although the group consists of two sub-groups, there is, nevertheless, unity and coherence. The trees grow vigorously, which means that twice a year the foliage pads have to be pinched back heavily. Of all the trees in my collection, this ranks as one of the firm favorites.

you use more than 11 or 13 trees, it is less important to stick rigidly to the convention of odd numbers. This is because the eye will not be able to assimilate the exact number of trees in a large composition.

In a group planting each individual tree has a role to play, but at the same time, they must all be subordinate to the overall design of the group. In a successful group each tree should complement the others; no individual tree can conflict with the overall design. This concept of unity is perhaps the cardinal principle of group and forest design in bonsai.

ZELKOVA GROUP

Trees used for group planting can be fairly immature, and need not be of particularly good quality. **Right** These *Zelkova serrata* illustrate the kind of tree which is most suited to group planting. The trees have been produced from cuttings, which were all taken from the same tree. Although this is an ideal situation, it is by no means essential. The cuttings range between 38-60cm (15-24in) in height, all of them are fairly straight, and the oldest is no more than six years old. **Far right** Remove the trees from their flowerpots, and reduce the root ball to a bare minimum. Place the trees roughly in position, and study the effect.

It is usual, when designing a group, to place the main tree in the center and surround it by slightly shorter trees, forming a roughly conical shape. Here, the shorter trees have been placed behind the tallest trees, thus creating a sense of perspective. **Right** More trees are added. It may be necessary to cut away half the root ball from a tree, in order to position it close to another tree. **Far right** After several hours of rearranging each individual tree, they are now in their final positions. The entire group has been planted slightly off-center, and arranged so that they appear to radiate from the center like a fan. The trees can now be potted up by filling the container with compost. The finished group is shown on pp112-3.

CYPRESS GROUP

In contrast to the zelkova group, only five trees have been used here. The variety chosen is *Chamaecyparis andelyensis thyoides*. These trees are nearly 60cm (2ft) tall, and because they are so straight, the effect created by a group planting will be very stately.

Trees chosen for group plantings should have a single trunk. This particular tree has a double trunk, which means that one will have to be removed. Obviously, the thinner, shorter trunk is the one to be discarded.

Place the principal tree in the central position. Put a second tree next to it, and study the effect. All branches have been wired downward to give the impression of age.

Experiment with the positions of the other three trees until you have the best possible arrangement. Remember that the principal, or tallest tree must be in the center.

The final version of the cypress group project is reminiscent of a small cluster of trees at the edge of a much larger forest. The height of the trees has been emphasized by the downward wiring of all the individual branches. Note that the distance between each of the trees has been varied so that any appearance of uniformity, and hence of artificiality, is avoided.

盆栽

I changed my mind about
the final arrangement of
the zelkova group;
instead of arranging the
trees so that they fanned
outward, I planted them
in tiny clusters. The
central group is a cluster
of four trees, there is a
sub-group of three trees
on the left, and the four
remaining trees have
been grouped in pairs
toward the right. The
soil has been covered
with moss scraped off
the ground, which gives
the impression that the
group has been in
existence for years. Few
people would guess that
three hours before this
picture was taken, all the
trees were in separate
flowerpots.

113

Unity

Unity in group planting is a difficult concept to convey, and an even more difficult concept to put into practice. The overall shape of the group must be conical in appearance, almost giving the impression of a single tree. The individual trees can be viewed as being like the branches of this tree; thus each must be trained with the overall shape in mind.

Regardless of its size, a group must always have unity, otherwise it will not be successful. A large group may be split into a number of subsidiary groups, but even then, the composition as a whole must have a unifying feel behind it.

Designing a group

Group and forest plantings are extremely versatile in that they can convey a wide range of impressions and feelings. By careful composition and arrangement of perspective, a group can convey either an impression of distance, or a feeling of close proximity. The two types of group are known as the "distant view group", and the "near view group". All these visual effects can be created by careful placing of different sized trees in various positions in the pot.

The importance of unity cannot be overemphasized: whether a group consists of two trees or 21, it must convey a sense of unity. For groups consisting of a few trees (i.e. 2, 3, or 5), this is most easily achieved by planting them very closely together. Thus, a two-tree group should resemble a twin trunk tree, while a three- or five-tree group should look like a triple, or five-trunk tree.

Space is another very important factor in the composition of groups. The space between individual trees, the space between sub-groups of trees within the same composition, and the space left deliberately unfilled all have a design function. The spacing between the trees should never be absolutely uniform: varying the distances between trees will create different perspectives, and immediately give interest to the group.

PLANTING ON SLATE
Groups which are to be planted on flat rocks are started off in seed trays, so that the roots mesh together, and hold the soil. Normally, the trees only take six months to become established, after which they may be lifted out of the tray, and placed on slate. **Right** A group of young trident maples in a seed tray. **Far right** The trees have been lifted out of the tray and placed on a piece of slate.

Group plantings are often made on flat rocks, which are sometimes drilled through so that anchor wires can be attached. (Top) Weathered tufa, with moss growing on it, (bottom right) Cornish slate, (bottom left) Welsh slate.

Once a group has been created, it will require further refinement and attention over the years.
Above This Ezo spruce group, consisting of eight trees, was imported from Japan in the early 1960s. The trees are 50-60 years old, and the tallest is nearly 86cm (34in) high. Ezo spruce are vigorous trees and, as this picture shows, after a full season's growth they need to be thinned out.
Left The trees in the group have all been pruned quite heavily, and some of the branches have been wired down to keep them in position. In addition, I decided that a larger, unglazed, oval pot would enhance their overall appearance.

Left This forest planting of 11 larches on Cornish slate was made nine years ago. The trees are about 15-20 years old. The application of a high potash fertilizer from midsummer to early fall encourages the trees to cone regularly. The only other care required is constant watering and feeding during the growing season, and pinching back new shoots. During the winter, the twigs which have grown too long are cut back to the first, or second bud of the current season's growth; occasionally they have to be cut back hard. **Above** This five-larch group was planted in a large seed tray earlier this year. The tallest tree is 90cm (36in), and about 15 years old. The group is fairly well established, and the roots will be able to hold the soil together, which means that the group can be planted on a rock, or placed in a shallow bonsai container. All the trees have been producing cones for the past four to five years.

STARTING A LARCH FOREST

Right These larches have been grown in open ground for seven to eight years. Three years ago they were cut back to half their height of 60-90cm (3-4ft). Two years ago they were lifted from the field, and potted up in 13cm (5in) and 18cm (7in) flowerpots. Potting up helps to restrict the roots, which means they can be readily used in group plantings. Trees selected for groups should be fairly straight, otherwise you will not be able to achieve the required effect. **Below left** Select a suitable seed tray. Here, I have used one that is 86 x 28cm (34 x 11in). Position the principal tree so that it is roughly in the center. Arrange the subsidiary trees around the central tree. The robin perched on the seed tray conveniently provides some indication of the group's size. **Bottom right** Two more trees have been placed in the tray – all fairly close together.

Left Smaller trees have been placed on one side to provide a contrast with the taller trees in the center of the group. **Above** The final arrangement uses 11 trees. During the growing season the branches will all be trimmed. and further refined. Next year, the group can be transferred to a slate, or placed in a large bonsai container. In a couple of year's time they will form a very pleasing forest planting.

Above This is part of a very large group of Chinese elm, which is being grown over a piece of artificial rock, made from glass-fiber. Most of the trees were produced from air layerings. Note how a sense of perspective has been created by planting larger trees in front, and smaller ones at the side, and at the back. The group is seen to best effect in winter when the trees are without leaves. **Right** This lovely group of Korean hornbeams was imported from Japan three years ago. Large numbers of groups such as this are produced in Japan. Beautifully composed, it exemplifies all the aesthetic qualities which should be present in a well-designed group – balance, perspective, movement, depth, and vitality.

Groups and sub-groups

There are two basic approaches to composing groups: grouping all the trees together in a single clump; and forming several sub-groups. Sub-groups can be used for any group planting consisting of five, or more trees. Thus, a five-tree group may consist of two sub-groups of three and two, while a seven-tree group could be composed of two groups of four and three, and so on.

As the number of trees in the group increases, so too can the number of sub-groups. However, you should not exceed five sub-groups, or the result will be confusing, rather than pleasing.

There are also two basic ways of arranging trees in a group: they may fan out from a central point, so that the trees almost resemble the rays of the sun; alternatively, all the trees can be grown upright (*see p111*). By now, it should be clear that the permutations of group plantings are endless, and that the impressions created will be infinite. This is one of the reasons why group design is such a challenging aspect of bonsai.

Group planting templates

When you first start to compose group or forest plantings, you may feel daunted by the prospect of choosing a suitable arrangement for the number of trees you have available. These templates are intended to guide you towards producing groups which are aesthetically pleasing. It is important to start with your principal tree, which is nearly always the largest one. Position the trees in sequence, choosing the correct size as indicated. Once you have mastered these arrangements, you will have enough confidence to create your own designs. The possibilities presented by group planting are infinite.

Two-tree groups

Three-tree groups

Five-tree groups

Varieties of tree

By tradition, groups are usually planted with a single variety of tree. There is a good horticultural reason for this: different species grow at varying rates, and the more vigorous variety would soon dominate the group. However, this is not insurmountable; if a variety grows too strongly, it can be replaced. In the meantime, the group can be enjoyed for at least a couple of years.

There is a wide choice of trees suitable for single variety groups. Some of the most popular are: Trident maple, Japanese maple, beech, hornbeam, larch, zelkova, stewartia, needle juniper and Chinese juniper. However, mixed groups combining species such as beech and Japanese maple are becoming increasingly common.

In conclusion, there are no hard and fast rules in group planting, because a living art form, such as bonsai, is constantly evolving. If one were to be too rigid, creativity would be stifled, there would be no advances in technique, and thus no new concepts of the art.

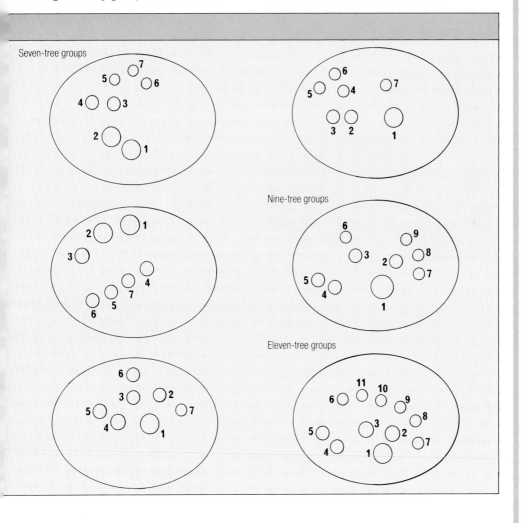

Seven-tree groups

Nine-tree groups

Eleven-tree groups

10

Planting on rocks

From a very early stage of Chinese civilization, mountains were believed to be the traditional dwelling places of the Chinese sages and mythical gods. It is not surprising, therefore, that mountains were regarded as sacred; indeed generations of Chinese have worshipped and venerated them. Rocks are considered to represent mountains, and thus have immense symbolic significance.

This special feeling about mountains and rocks has meant that they influence almost every facet of Chinese art, literature and religion. You need only to look at Chinese painting to realize that no landscape is considered complete, unless mountains are featured in some way or another. In fact, the very expression for landscape painting in Chinese is *san-sui*, which means "mountain and water". To this day, Chinese painting, garden design and *pen-jing*, or potted landscapes, all revolve around the symbolic use of rocks. Without rocks, a work of art is considered to be devoid of the power and grandeur which is associated with mountains.

In time, as with most of the Oriental arts which originated in China, such as painting, calligraphy, ceramics and garden art, this love of mountains and rocks spread via Korea to Japan, where it developed in new and imaginative ways.

This dramatic Suiseki was photographed on a recent visit to China, and is reminiscent of craggy mountain scenery.

Rocks in Bonsai

The art of using rocks in bonsai, therefore, must be seen in the context of its historical and religious significance. In essence, this means that rocks symbolize mountains. Understanding this concept not only provides a multitude of compositional possibilities, but also broadens the viewer's appreciation of the aesthetics of bonsai.

Including rocks in a bonsai composition enhances the illusion of miniaturized reality. A piece of rock can be used to denote either an entire

This composition was created 15 years ago, using a larch sapling collected from the wild, and is intended to give the impression of a tree clinging to a rocky precipice. Some of the roots have been fixed to the rock by attaching tiny anchor wires to the surface with epoxy resin. The other roots have been draped over the rock, enabling them to grow into the soil. The tree is about 30-40 years old, and 60cm (24in) high. The fine ramification of the branches has been achieved by constant pinching of the growing tips over many years.

mountain, or part of a mountain: for example, a tree planted on a rock may suggest a tree growing out of a high cliff. There is no need for a representation of the entire mountain; it is enough to visualize the tree jutting from a rocky ledge.

The aesthetic and symbolic connotations associated with rocks reach a deeper level when the association with mountains is no longer necessary. Instead, the rock is admired for its intrinsic

beauty – it is a work of art in its own right. In some respects, this is the principle behind the viewing stones, or *sui-sek* (Chinese for "water stone"), which are described in more detail in a later chapter (*see pp138-43*).

At this stage, however, it is more useful to think of the rocks used in bonsai as representing mountains. By skilful planting of trees on different types of rock, you can achieve very pleasing effects. In fact, such a composition can be quite stunning.

JUNIPERS ON ROCK

Right This striking composition of Chinese junipers on Westmorland rock was made 15 years ago. The intention was to create a cascade of trees on a single piece of rock, emulating the way junipers tend to grow in the wild. To create such a group, you must first find a suitable piece of rock, preferably with an interesting surface texture. Ideally, the rock should stand up vertically, rather than lie horizontally; a vertical rock has much greater impact, and will give the impression of a mountain in miniature. It is important not to conceal the interesting features of the rock, otherwise it will lose much of its beauty. This particular rock has been sawn off, giving it a flat base.

Glue lengths of green plastic-covered garden wire to the rock with a strong epoxy resin. Use the anchor wires to tie the roots tightly to the rock surface. Smear a clayey compost over the rocks to keep the root ball and compost intact.

Over the years the roots have anchored themselves to the rock, and meshed together. This composition is usually displayed in a *sui-ban*, giving the impression of a rocky precipice overlooking the sea.

Left This Japanese root-over-rock trident maple is about 15-20 years old. Such compositions take years to create: it could be 6-8 years before the roots even clasp the rock. Not surprisingly, such trees are very expensive. The objective is to convey the impression of a tree growing among rocks in the high mountains.

Above This large piece of Westmorland rock would not look as impressive if it were horizontal; therefore, it has been set vertically in a slab of concrete. The base can be camouflaged with moss, or embedded in a bonsai pot.

Tufa rock makes a very attractive base for a small composition. It is a soft rock which can be carved fairly easily, which means that small crevices can be hollowed out, filled with soil, and planted. **Left** A chunk of tufa rock planted with miniature rhododendrons and pines. Rock plantings such as this should be kept moist throughout the summer as the little trees do not stand up to drought well. Keep in a shady position, and water it at least twice a day during hot weather.

Above top This close-up of tufa rock planted with moss, miniature thyme, and rhododendron shows how the surface texture enhances the plants. **Above** These rocks will be used for tree-over-rock compositions. From the left: Westmorland stone, tufa, Westmorland stone, and tufa. Moss softens the appearance of rocks, giving them a more natural look. Anchor wires have already been positioned on some of them, and will be used to help anchor small trees to the rocks.

Right A trident maple which I have been training over a rock for the past four years. Initially, the tree was only 37mm in diameter, but it has increased to nearly 10cm (4in). It spent the first three years in the ground, and was then transferred to a large plastic pot.

Right The fine fibrous roots have been scraped away, revealing that the main roots are just beginning to clasp the rock. Plastic-covered copper wire has been used to tie the roots to the rock. Every other year the tree is lifted from the ground for inspection, and refinement. In a couple of years' time, the top of the tree, which is now 2.4m (8ft) high will be sawn off, and the final bonsai design developed.

ROOT-OVER-ROCK BONSAI

Creating a good root-over-rock bonsai can take many years. It is partly for this reason that the varieties of tree chosen for such compositions tend to be fast-growing. Thus the favorite subjects are trident and mountain maples.

Above top A three-year-old trident maple grown from a cutting. Note the long fibrous roots. **Above** Although the thick roots might seem ugly, they can be turned into a feature.

Far left View the tree from different directions until you have decided on the most attractive profile. **Left** This is probably the most interesting aspect of the trident maple. If it is planted on the rock in this position, the thick base will show to best advantage.

Above Find a suitable piece of rock -one that will match the shape of the tree's base.

Above Place the tree on the rock so that it fits snugly into the rock surface. Tie it in position with soft plastic string. Do not cut off any of the fine roots as the tree needs these to survive. **Left** Once the tree has been tied to the rock, it can be planted in a large plastic seed tray. The tree can be left to grow for the next few years. Alternatively, it can be planted in the ground.

11 Chinese-style bonsai

An original woodcut attributed to Hiroshige, entitled "View of Hara from the Tokaido Road". It is not known why the artist depicted this landscape in a ceramic pot, but I like to think that it is a piece of "potted landscape" very much in the tradition of Chinese *pen-jing*. Certainly, this beautifully-composed picture is a fitting inspiration for any bonsai artist.

To the connoisseur, Chinese bonsai has a style of its own. In fact, it is totally different from the bonsai generally seen in the West today. The main reason for this is that the art of bonsai in China has hardly changed over the last seventy to eighty years.

At the turn of the century Chinese and Japanese bonsai were much alike, but whereas Japanese bonsai has developed considerably, Chinese bonsai has remained virtually the same. Photographs of Japanese bonsai, taken in London in 1902 at the first exhibition of dwarf trees ever held in the West, reveal styles which are almost indistinguishable from those of Chinese bonsai today. It is true to say, therefore, that the art of Chinese bonsai has not been influenced by developments anywhere in the world, particularly in Japan.

The Cultural Revolution is mainly responsible for this isolation from outside influence. China was completely closed to the West between 1949 and the late 1970s. In addition, bonsai was considered a very bourgeois and revisionist pastime, which was frowned upon by the authorities. As a result, the art of bonsai nearly died out. Fortunately, the Chinese people were intelligent enough not to throw bonsai overboard, just because politicians told them to do so. Ironically, it was the ordinary working class people and peasants who continued to practice bonsai, unbeknown to the authorities. In this respect, bonsai was truly a proletarian art.

Happily for the rest of the world, bonsai in China survived that difficult period, and is flourishing once again. There is a developing trade in bonsai between China and Western countries, which should stimulate interest in the West for the Chinese style of tree. Indeed, the West stands to gain much from the ancient and distinguished tradition of Chinese bonsai.

盆栽

Chinese-style bonsai
were rarely seen outside
China until a few years
ago. This *Vitex chinensis*
is reputed to be well over
100 years old, and is
60cm (24in) high. The
contorted trunk and
squiggly branches are
typically Chinese, giving
the tree an almost
abstract quality. In late
summer, it produces tiny
mauve flowers. The tree
was shown at London's
Chelsea Flower Show in
1980 and, attracted by
its unique qualities, I
added it to my collection.

Chinese schools

Although Chinese bonsai as a whole
have a distinctive character, several
schools or styles are recognized within
China itself. Each school has its own
style: the bonsai grown in the north are
different from those in the south; while
the growers in the west have a totally
different approach from those of the
east. These regional differences include
pots, which vary in style, color and
shape; and tree varieties. The growers in
the south, for instance, make extensive
use of Fukien tea (*Carmona* species),
Chinese elm (*Ulmus parviflora*) and Bird
plum cherry (*Sageretia*), while the
growers in the north concentrate on
Podocarpus, and pines. Visitors to China
should bear these differences in mind.

133

Landscapes such as this piece of mountain scenery made from tufa rock, are typically Chinese. Although mass produced, each composition is very realistic. The display pot has been specially made for it. Little plants and trees may be grown in the crevices of the rock. Some people use these landscapes as humidifiers: the container is filled with water, which is then drawn up through the porous rock, and released into the atmosphere.

Comparing Chinese and Japanese styles

In general, in comparison with contemporary Japanese bonsai, Chinese bonsai is less refined. There is more informality and less attention to detail, particularly in specimen trees; extensive use is made of exposed roots, and the contorted shapes of trunks and branches. The love of beautiful rocks, which is such a strong tradition in China, is reflected in all their bonsai, as well as their *pen-jing*.

One of the most pleasing aspects of Chinese bonsai, however, is their impressionistic appearance. The *pen-jing*, or landscape bonsai, in particular, strongly resemble the brushstroke paintings of the literati and zen schools. The freedom and informality of these compositions have a freshness which is probably unique in bonsai art. The influence of Chinese painting is perhaps most clearly seen in their cascade and literati style trees, which have a most unusual and refreshing quality; the sharp angular shape of the trunk, and the sweeping curves of the branches, recalling the brushstokes peculiar to Chinese painting.

Rocks in Chinese Bonsai

The skilful use of rocks by Chinese bonsai artists, has been unashamedly copied by the Japanese. In fact, the Japanese fascination for *suiseki*, or Viewing Stones, is of Chinese origin.

Chinese rock plantings come in various shapes and sizes, ranging from a few centimeters high to one, or even two meters (3-6ft). These exquisite, and very realistic creations can be planted with small trees, or with other accent planting material. They are intended to convey the impression of natural landscape scenery, rather than to highlight beautiful trees.

When rocks are combined with bonsai trees, the composition takes on a completely different feeling. This is where Chinese bonsai is so different from its Japanese counterpart. These compositions do not necessarily depend on superb trees, since it is the overall effect which is of primary importance. Sometimes both the rocks and the trees are equally beautiful, but somehow neither dominates or overshadows the other; there is a unity which is achieved by very skilful handling of the material. Many Chinese rock scenes are made up of composite pieces, which are glued or cemented together. This technique produces some very pleasing effects, especially when combined with the Chinese tradition of displaying rock scenes on beautiful marble trays filled with water.

Trunks and roots

Chinese artists have a predilection for trees with rugged or weirdly-shaped trunks. In fact, some go to great lengths to produce what would be regarded in the West as unnatural shapes. Exposed roots and gnarled, hollowed-out trunks are a popular way of accentuating the feeling of great age. Dead wood, too, is used, although not necessarily jinned, as in Japan.

Varieties of tree

The Chinese use nearly 200 varieties of tree for bonsai, most of which are also employed by Japanese bonsai artists. However, in general, the varieties with very small leaves are the most popular.

The practice of creating bonsai from collected trees is, of course, not new to the Chinese, who have been collecting them for centuries, but collected trees are not as highly valued as in Japan. Many of the trees collected in China are

stumps of old trees, which have been coppiced for years by villagers collecting firewood.

Air layering, which originated in China, continues to be practiced, and is still an important method for propagating trees.

The distinct differences between Chinese and Japanese bonsai should not be viewed in a critical or negative light. On the contrary, such differences, which widen the spectrum of styles and techniques, can only enrich the art of bonsai.

Not all rock landscapes originate from China: these two pieces of carboniferous limestone were collected from a rocky coast in Wales. The tallest rock is 40cm (16in) high; both have been set in cement so that they stand vertically. The harsh lines of the rocks have been softened by planting plants such as ferns and little alpines.

This elm started life as a
sucker taken from a
suburban hedge; the
entire canopy has
developed over the past
five years. As the tree
has thickened, and the
branches have become
more refined, it has
taken on a character of
its own. Planted in a
"Chinese" style, it gives
the impression of a tree
on a rocky hillside.

盆栽

An original woodcut by Hiroshige entitled " View of Kawasaki from the Tokaido Road". It appears to depict the busy life in a picturesque, little village by the riverside; and yet it remains a mystery to me why the artist has set the entire picture in a flowerpot. Perhaps it reflects the Chinese passion for miniature landscape, which developed into "Saikei" or Tray landscape.

The focus of this woodcut by Hiroshige, entitled "View of Kanaya from the Tokaido Road", is a magnificent tree. Trees such as this provided the models for bonsai, while the rocks resemble the Ibigawa rocks used for root-over-rock trees.

12

Suiseki

To the uninitiated, a piece of rock placed in a shallow bonsai dish filled with sand or water is often a source of great amusement. At exhibitions where fine Suiseki were displayed, I have often heard cynical, or disparaging remarks, made either from ignorance, or because the viewer's aesthetic sense had not been trained to appreciate their beauty. This attitude is unfortunate because there is so much enjoyment to be gained from looking at Suiseki. Beautiful rocks are like pieces of sculpture; the only difference is that they have been created by nature over millions of years, rather than by man.

The appreciation of Suiseki is very similar to the appreciation of classical music. Just as a Beethoven symphony is not to everyone's taste, so too Suiseki tends to appeal to a limited audience. To appreciate Suiseki one must acquire a taste for it. What, then, is Suiseki, and why does it evoke such strong emotions in many people?

Origins of Suiseki

Since ancient times, the Chinese have admired beautiful rocks. Rocks symbolized mountains, and for the Chinese, mountains were the embodiment of virtually every mystical and aesthetic experience imaginable.

The Chinese used rocks extensively in their landscape gardens to represent mountains, just as painters would employ mountain scenery to evoke a sense of the majestic in their paintings. The Chinese expression for landscape, whether in the context of painting or gardening, is *San Sui*, which means "mountain and water". The rocks in their compositions were known as *San Sui-sek*, or "stones used for landscape". Over the centuries, the full expression *San-Sui-Sek* has become abbreviated to *Sui-Sek* or "water stone".

Although the Chinese have always

This Suiseki reminds the viewer of mountain cliffs, illustrating the Chinese reverence for beautiful rocks.

盆栽

This typical Chinese miniature rock landscape is made from "Wu Cai Fu Pi" stone. The composition is 20cm (8in) high and 34cm (13in) wide. The pieces of rock have been carefully selected to achieve harmony and balance. The rocks were then cut and shaped with hand chisels, glued together using a cement which would blend with the color of the rocks, and set in a marble tray. If desired, it may be planted with small grasses, and other suitable plants.

admired rocks, there was a period, around the Tang Dynasty, when almost the entire nation was obsessed with collecting interesting and beautifully-shaped rocks. Rocks of all sizes and shapes, both large and small, were collected, either for their intrinsic beauty, or simply because it was the fashion. It was out of this obsession that the true tradition of Suiseki emerged.

The appreciation of rocks for their intrinsic beauty only reached Japan about five or six hundred years ago, and yet, as with most Oriental arts copied from the Chinese, the Japanese soon excelled at it. Whereas the Chinese used rocks mainly to symbolize mountains, the Japanese have developed a more imaginative approach. Over the years, they have learned to interpret beautiful stones in many different ways, such as islands, tortoises, waterfalls and bridges.

More recently, the Japanese have introduced a new type of viewing stone, known as the "chrysanthemum stone" or *Kikka-seki*. These are large, very smooth rocks, with beautiful chrysanthemum patterns embedded in them. Such stones are greatly admired, and highly prized.

Choosing stones

The true viewing stone is almost abstract in its quality; the viewer has to use his, or her, imagination to interpret and absorb its full significance. The Chinese, on the other hand, are less subtle in their approach: their rocks closely resemble the shapes and textures of mountains seen in nature.

The Chinese make extensive use of slates, which represent the mountains of central and western China. These mountain stones can range from a few centimeters to one or two meters (3-6ft) in height, and they come in a variety of colors – pink, gray or white.

In the West very little use has been made of indigenous stones for viewing

I found these two massive pieces of ironstone by the roadside in Hampshire, England. They were about to be crushed by a bulldozer for roadfill when I spotted them. I collected several pieces, but only these two lent themselves to this particular composition, which is reminiscent of a deep canyon. Moss and lichen grow well on this rock, but are never allowed to obscure the lovely texture of the rock face.

This rock is from the island of Barra, off the Scottish coast. A beautiful, blue-gray stone, with a hint of mauve, it has been sculpted by years of exposure to the waves. Although far from the sea, it still conveys the feeling of a rocky cliff battered by waves.

This beautiful Suiseki is a perfect miniature of a rocky mountain. The base has been cut flat, and a special wooden stand has been made for displaying it.

purposes. This is a shame, because there is such a wealth of rocks throughout the world which would make excellent viewing stones. In almost every country, it must be possible to find rocks which could easily rival the beauty of the Chinese and Japanese Suiseki. The examples illustrated of indigenous material collected in Britain, are by no means outstanding, but I hope they will encourage you to become more interested in this aspect of bonsai.

In order to make the best use of local material for Suiseki, select rocks that most closely resemble those used by the Chinese and Japanese. Most good books on Japanese and Chinese bonsai will contain pictures of such stones.

Many rocks offer tremendous scope for use as viewing stones, but are discarded because they are considered to be either too bulky or too unstable for display. There are two ways of overcoming these drawbacks. The first is to fix the rock in the desired position with cement or synthetic glue. Epoxy resin, or

car filler paste (a type of fiberglass resin) are excellent for this purpose, as is quick-setting cement. Alternatively, large pieces of rock can be set in a bed of concrete, which can then be fitted into a bonsai pot.

If the second method does not appeal to you, then you might consider creating a flat base with a grinding wheel or a cutting disk. Slate and sandstone are fairly easy materials to shape with a cutting disk, but for harder rocks, such as granite or marble, you may need to use diamond cutting tools.

Displaying Suiseki

Viewing stones are admired and exhibited as works of art in their own right. Consequently, they are always displayed in isolation.

There are two methods of displaying Suiskei: in shallow bonsai dishes filled with either sand, gravel, or even water; or on a stand, which has been specially carved to fit the shape of the stone. As

Above This "hut-shaped rock" is in fact a fossil, found in Shropshire, England. Fossils are ideal subjects for Suiseki as some of them have lovely shapes and textures. I have tried to combine fossils with some of my very old trees, but I have yet to achieve a satisfactory composition in which both fossil and tree appear as a unified whole. In most cases, one becomes the focus of attention, diminishing the intrinsic beauty of the other. **Left** Ironstone has a particularly lovely texture, which is displayed to maximum advantage by mounting it vertically.

with bonsai, you will need to establish the best viewing side for each piece of rock, so that it can be displayed to its best advantage.

The simplest way of displaying viewing stones is to place them in a shallow bonsai tray filled with sand or gravel. If you can find a shallow tray without drainage holes (known as *sui-ban* or "water basin") this can be filled with water. If you are good at carving wood, or you know a woodcarver, then you might consider making an individual stand, which will enhance the rock, giving it an added elegance.

Although large viewing stones are best displayed on their own, Suiseki will complement large specimen bonsai in much the same way that accent plantings are used to contrast with specimen trees.

13

Exhibiting bonsai

As you become more interested in bonsai, and your collection of trees increases, it is natural that you should wish to exhibit them. There is immense pleasure and satisfaction to be gained from exhibiting your trees. Not only does it allow you to share the work of art you have created with a wider audience, but you will gain great pleasure from knowing that your handiwork is being admired by others.

There are many opportunities for showing bonsai. At the simplest level, you could organize a little bonsai show yourself, using local facilities such as a church or community hall. Bonsai clubs tend to organize local shows, which enable their members to display their best trees. In addition, clubs may become involved with horticultural shows, or national bonsai exhibitions.

In most countries, there are countless flower shows, both in the big cities and in the provinces. These tend to be held in the summer in temperate countries, and in the winter in the tropics. Clubs, nurseries and individuals are usually encouraged to exhibit at these events because of the public interest in bonsai. The same is true of hobby and specialist exhibitions.

There are two approaches to exhibiting bonsai: as individual trees forming part of an exhibition of bonsai trees only; and as an integrated bonsai display, which forms part of a general gardening exhibition. The former is very popular in Japan, while the latter is more common in the West. This distinction is important because the presentation of the display will depend largely on the nature of the exhibition concerned.

Bonsai exhibitions

When you enter trees for an exhibition which consists entirely of bonsai, the individual qualities of the bonsai are of

Bonsai form an integral part of this beautiful little garden. Almost every tree is a specimen bonsai, and they are displayed on oak benches about 1m (3ft) high.

盆栽

prime importance. This is partly because each tree will be selected purely on its individual merits, and partly because bonsai enthusiasts will be viewing each tree with a critical eye, assessing it for its special qualities. Thus, although the overall presentation is important, the quality of the individual trees is paramount.

General exhibitions

If your tree is being shown as part of a general display of bonsai at a flower show, such as the Chelsea Flower Show in London, then the trees forming the bonsai exhibit should be regarded as a single entity. This means that you should select trees of different sizes, shapes, colors, and textures, so that they blend with each other to create an overall effect, which is both pleasing and attractive.

In recent years, an increasing number of bonsai exhibitions held in Western countries are being staged in prestigious art galleries, and similar venues. This is a most encouraging trend, as it reflects the growing recognition of bonsai as a true art form.

Preparing for exhibition

It goes without saying that trees for exhibition must be in prime horticultural condition; there is nothing worse than a fine tree in poor show condition. It is vital for the trees to be healthy: foliage must be fresh, green and vigorous; if they are in blossom, the flowers should be just about to bloom; fall color should be perfect.

Grooming a tree for exhibition can be very time consuming; it could take you as long as 12 hours to groom a large specimen tree for a show.

Foliage

When grooming a pine, all the downward pointing needles need to be removed, as do all needles which are superfluous to any particular branch. With Japanese

A view of my old needle juniper (see previous page) before grooming. Needle junipers are prolific growers, and require constant pinching of new shoots. Some owners allow their trees to grow without interference for certain periods in order to encourage vigor; others keep them constantly groomed and pinched. Both approaches are acceptable, provided you feed and water the tree properly. Refinement is ultimately a question of aesthetics.

black pines, you should be meticulous about removing unwanted needles in order to give the tree a fresh and airy appearance. Chinese junipers need very heavy pinching to remove the coarse growth, as well as any growth outside the foliage mounds.

In the case of deciduous trees, remove all dead leaves, as well as those which have been scorched or shrivelled by the wind, or the sun.

Branches

Attention to detail should not be confined to the condition and color of the foliage; the structure and refinement of the branches are just as important. Any branch or twig which is in the wrong position should be removed or rewired, so that it does not spoil the overall design. The shape of the tree, whether conical, or round, must be meticulously refined until it looks neat and tidy.

Trunks

If trunks are not cleaned regularly, they tend to collect algae; a neglected trunk can become completely covered in moss. It is a good idea to clean the trunk and branches regularly, using a stiff brush, such as a toothbrush, and a mild detergent, or else just plain water. When cleaning trees with rough bark, such as pines, be careful not to damage the flaky bark. Chinese junipers have a lovely, smooth, reddish bark, which looks particularly attractive when it has been properly cleaned. Some Japanese exhibitors enhance the color of juniper bark with brown shoe polish. However, in my opinion, this is unnecessary.

Driftwood

Trees with a large amount of driftwood should be treated regularly with lime sulphur; preferably about two months before the trees are due to be displayed. The white, bleached effect is more pleasing if it is allowed to weather slightly; while some recommend mixing a little Indian ink in the lime sulphur to tone down the whiteness.

Moss

Moss which is growing naturally in the pot is more effective than moss which has been freshly dug up and placed on the surface of the soil. You can encourage moss to grow by sprinkling powdered moss on the surface, and then watering it constantly. There are several varieties, but the fine emerald moss is the best. Once the covering of moss has become too thick, it should be removed, and you should start growing a new covering from scratch.

The shape and size of a pot can dramatically alter the overall appearance of a bonsai. A pot is just like a picture frame; a beautiful tree can be ruined by an inappropriate pot. For the last ten years this Japanese black pine has been growing in a deep, square pot. I decided it would look better in a traditional, rectangular pot. Here, it is being positioned in a pot specially made by Gordon Duffett.

All trees need to be groomed and refined from time to time, especially if they are to be exhibited. Pines, in particular, need meticulous grooming, otherwise they look ragged and untidy. As a general rule, all downward pointing needles on a pine should be removed. **Above left** An unrefined branch. **Above right** The downward pointing needles have been removed. **Right** Each downward pointing needle should be carefully plucked, using your thumb and forefinger. On a large pine this can take several hours, but the result is quite spectacular.

When making a bonsai, one of the aims is to create the illusion of a real tree in miniature form. **Right** This massive Chinese juniper is believed to be well over 100 years old. It has large areas of dead driftwood, particularly near the base, which means that very few surface roots remain. **Above** Deciding that the appearance of the tree would be improved by adding some roots, I found a piece of dead juniper, which would blend with the existing trunk, and give the appearance of an authentic root.

Rocks and accent plantings

Small rocks can enhance the beauty of a tree considerably, particularly if the tree has minor faults at the trunk base, or if the roots are not very attractive. For instance, an ugly root can be hidden, or even camouflaged, by placing an interesting piece of rock in just the right position.

Accent plantings, such as thyme, rush, acorus, and dwarf irises, perform a very similar function. They can also be planted in small, shallow bonsai dishes and used to complement large trees.

Timing

It is important to time your preparation so that the trees reach their peak condition just as the show begins. There are various ways in which you can control the appearance of your trees.

If maples are being shown to display their beautiful spring leaves, they can be encouraged to come into leaf under controlled conditions in a cool greenhouse. This will also prevent any scorching of their foliage by frost or wind. On the other hand, if fine fall color is desired, trees can be fertilized appropriately during the summer, and then exposed to fall frosts in order to induce the colors. Bright green coloring can be induced by applying the right amount of high nitrogen fertilizer some four to six weeks before the trees are to be shown. Excessive sunlight is not desirable for evergreens as it causes slight yellowing of the foliage,

A bird's eye view of a branch of one of my specimen trident maples, showing the fine ramification of twigs that has been developed over the years. This has been achieved by constant pinching and pruning of the branches. Deciduous trees, such as trident maple and zelkova, are traditionally displayed during the winter when they are without their foliage. It is only then that their intricate branch structure can be fully appreciated.

Many potential bonsai lack a substantial trunk. However, it is possible to thicken trunks in a number of ways. **Right** Carefully score the bark with a knife. **Below left** Alternatively, knock the bark with a stout hammer from time to time. **Below right** Scoring this Scots pine has allowed the trunk to expand.

Right The air-layering techniques of ring-barking and tourniquet will cause a trunk to swell, and even encourage a pleasing taper. They can also be applied to encourage a good flare at the base of a tree. In time, roots will form where the sap flow has been restricted. This technique is often used to create a new set of roots, and thus to eliminate bad roots.

whereas keeping them in a slightly shady position will enhance the green coloring.

Many deciduous trees are best shown during the winter, or dormant season, when they are without their leaves. It is only then that the beautiful tracery of their branches can be seen to full advantage. Mountain maples, trident maples, and zelkova, in particular, are at their most elegant without leaves; the same trees in full leaf are just a mass of foliage, the branch structure cannot be seen, and the overall effect is not as graceful, or sophisticated; consequently this is the traditional season for exhibiting them. Maples, however, are also much appreciated for their fall color.

Display stands and pots

The traditional way of displaying bonsai is with a special display stand. If you look at ancient Chinese and Japanese manuscripts and scrolls, bonsai are invariably displayed in this way. Even today, at major Japanese and Chinese exhibitions, all trees, regardless of size, are always displayed complete with antique, carved, wooden stands.

Antique Chinese and Japanese wooden display stands are ideal for enhancing a display of bonsai. However, they should be simple and restrained in design, otherwise they will detract from the beauty of the trees themselves. Flat pieces of wood cut from large tree trunks can also make very effective stands. Alternatively, you can make simple display boxes of wood, painted in a neutral color, or covered with either felt or burlap.

When you display your trees, always make sure that the pots are not broken or cracked in any way – this is a detail which is often overlooked. The emphasis should always be to ensure that the trees are immaculate in every way – from the condition of the foliage to the color of the moss.

If you are going to the trouble of displaying your trees, it is worth putting on the best show possible. You should never be satisfied with second best; after all, both the judges and the viewing public deserve the very best. The judges, in particular, will be looking for faults, so anything you can do to minimize that opportunity will stand you in good stead.

One hardly needs to stress the importance of transporting and handling a tree with care. After all, you need only damage one branch of a show tree to ruin years of careful work for some considerable time to come.

Viewing height

Most bonsai exhibits are best viewed at waist or eye level, hence the optimum height for display tables is between 76-90cm (30-36ins). Variation in the height of the actual trees can be achieved by placing them on wooden display stands, or plinths, on the tables.

Insuring your trees

It is always wise to insure your trees against theft, damage and vandalism when they are on public display. Many people also install sophisticated security alarm systems in their gardens. Always keep a photographic record of your trees, as this will help in tracing them. If a tree is stolen, immediately notify the police, bonsai dealers, and clubs.

However, do not allow yourself to become overly worried about theft. By and large the vast majority of the public are honest, and sensible security measures will reduce the opportunity for theft considerably.

REFINING A BONSAI
Right This hawthorn was developed by a blind bonsai grower. She shaped and developed the tree by feel over 25 years. By growing it in a tiny square bonsai pot, the roots had no room for expansion, and have therefore acquired an attractive, gnarled appearance. **Far right** The tree was brought to me for improvement. My first suggestion was to place it in a much larger oval pot, which would be more in proportion to the tree. Simply changing the pot has already transformed the tree's appearance.

Right Next, I removed the crossing branches, and the twin leader. Note how the branches are now arranged in more logical tiers than was previously the case. Over the next few years the branch ramification will be encouraged to develop in the flat foliage pads that have been created **Far right** Changing the viewing angle of the tree gives it a more natural appearance, while the addition of a large piece of rock provides a counterbalance to the interesting root structure. These pictures show the transforming effect minor branch refinement, or repotting, can have on a tree's appearance.

14 The international scene

It goes without saying that the best bonsai exhibitions are held in Japan. The exhibition season opens in mid-November with the National Diet Bonsai Exhibition. It is held in the Kensei Memorial Hall near the Diet Building in Tokyo, and is visited by most of the important political figures in Japan.

The next major exhibition is the Nippon Bonsai Taikan Exhibition (or Grand View Bonsai Exhibition), which is normally held during the last week in November and the first week of December. It claims to be the largest and most comprehensive bonsai exhibition in Japan, and comprises 450 trees, as well as Suiseki.

In the third week of January the Nippon Bonsai Sakufu Exhibition is staged at the famous Daimaru Department Store in Tokyo. The exhibition is for the professional bonsai artists of Japan, and, by tradition, is the opportunity for them to present their latest works. Once trees have been shown here, they become quite famous, and their value increases considerably.

During the second week in February the Kokofu Bonsai Exhibition is held in the Tokyo Metropolitan Art Museum. An annual exhibition like most of the others, it has been held since 1934, and is both the longest established bonsai exhibition and the most prestigious. Approximately 200-300 trees are shown. The entrance qualifications are very high and normally only about half of the trees entered manage to qualify for display. Bonsai enthusiasts would regard having their work displayed at this show as the achievement of a lifetime ambition. And, as always, the value of a tree increases dramatically once it has been selected.

In the last week of April to the first week of May, the International Bonsai and Suiseki Exhibition is held in Senri in Osaka at the famous Expo'70 Commemoration Park. It is organized by the Nippon Bonsai Association and

盆栽

This red Deshojo maple is grown in the twin-trunk style, and is 84cm (33in) high. In general, twin-trunk trees are planted with both trunks in full view. However, by placing the smaller tree so that it is slightly offset behind the larger tree, the composition is given a better perspective.

sponsored by the Ministries of Foreign Affairs and Cultural Affairs. Photographs of trees from all over the world are included in the exhibition.

During the summer, in the second week of August, a special exhibition of 100-500 Suiseki is held at the Mitsukoshi Department Store in Tokyo.

Japanese bonsai exhibitions are so popular that lengthy queues are inevitable; nevertheless visiting any one of these shows is an experience to remember. In addition, a commemorative album, featuring the trees displayed, is usually produced for each exhibition. Such albums are invaluable for any bonsai student; studying the pictures can provide inspiration, and point the way to improving your own trees.

Foreign visitors wanting more information about bonsai exhibitions in Japan should write to the Nippon Bonsai Association.

Exhibitions outside Japan

In China, formal bonsai exhibitions of the kind held in Japan are rare. Many of their bonsai displays are held in botanical gardens and recreational parks, mostly during the early spring at the time of the Chinese New Year. In Hong Kong, bonsai exhibitions are held fairly frequently in the City Hall.

The first recorded exhibition of miniature trees ever held in the West took place in London in 1902. Pictures of the exhibits from this famous show depict mostly Hinoki cypress, thuja, *Prunus mume*, *Prunus parviflora*, and trident maple. The styles are highly reminiscent of the Chinese style, and the trees were almost invariably planted in deep, circular pots. Semi cascade, informal upright, and exposed root were the most popular styles. There were also a number of tray landscapes, or *Bonkai*, on display; these were in shallow, rectangular pots.

The next time bonsai made an appearance was in 1910 at the "Britain-Japan Exhibition" in London. Other major exhibitions followed – the Paris Peace Exhibition in 1925, and the 1937 World Exhibition in Paris. Bonsai were not shown at the famous Chelsea Flower Show in London until 1960.

In the last eight to ten years, more and more bonsai exhibitions have been organized world wide. Enthusiasts should write to the national bonsai association of the country they intend visiting to obtain details of local shows.

Clubs and societies

There are bonsai clubs and societies now in almost every country. In Britain, for instance, there are some 20 major clubs in the large cities, numerous smaller clubs, and an umbrella organization called the Federation of British Bonsai Societies. Most European countries have local bonsai clubs, as well as a national organization. In addition, the European clubs combined in 1983 to form the European Bonsai Association which, among other matters, organizes regular bonsai conventions.

Clubs play a very useful role in promoting interest in bonsai. They disseminate knowledge, improve the standards of bonsai generally, and provide a venue for enthusiasts to meet and exchange ideas. Many clubs organize workshops, outings, and even visits to foreign countries.

I often receive letters from individuals complaining that there is no bonsai club near their home town. I can quite understand their frustration, but I normally advise them to take the initiative and start a club themselves. Nothing could be simpler than placing an advertisement in a local paper, or even writing an article to stimulate the interest of other readers. Many clubs have been started in this way: all it needs is for someone to start the ball rolling; there is no reason why it should not be you.

Visiting fellow enthusiasts

Although bonsai are seen at their best at special exhibitions and at flower shows, many enthusiasts enjoy viewing the collections of other individuals, especially when they are abroad. Most bonsai enthusiasts welcome such visits, and with some careful planning, you will find this can be a very rewarding experience.

Conventions

Conventions for bonsai enthusiasts are becoming increasingly popular. In America, several conventions are held each year in different parts of the country; in Europe and the United Kingdom conventions are held annually, or biannually. Such meetings usually last two or three days, and comprise speakers, and demonstrations of special techniques. Many conventions are now so international in flavor that they can be described as world conventions.

Commercial aspects

The growth of interest in bonsai in recent years, particularly in the West, has stimulated the commercial side of bonsai considerably. In almost every continent outside Asia, there are many wholesale and retail outlets specializing in bonsai trees and accessories. The Japanese have, of course, cornered the market for bonsai – both in trees and in the accessories. This is not just because of their superior marketing ability, but because the quality of their products is so high.

It is always worth making personal contact with dealers, whether in Japan, Hong Kong or China, before placing orders. It is not uncommon for agents to abscond with the money, without fulfilling their orders, or for consignments of pots to arrive as rubble because they have been so poorly packed. In general, the Japanese dealers are extremely honest, and the care and precision with which they pack their wares is quite amazing. The Chinese, unfortunately, tend not to have the same sophistication, which is a pity as some of their products are very handsome. A cardinal rule, therefore, is to be extremely careful in choosing suppliers.

Importing trees

Most countries have very strict rules about importing trees from abroad, and these should be adhered to meticulously. It is likely that extensive documentation and import permit arrangements will be required before the trees are allowed into the country. Thereafter, the trees will be quarantined for a specific period of time to ensure that they do not carry and spread disease to native plants. Certain countries, such as Australia and South Africa, have banned the importation of trees. Where such a ban exists, it is not worth trying to circumvent the rules.

The traditional way of paying for imports from China and Japan is by letter of credit. Any other means of payment is very risky; always consult your bank before embarking on projects which require extensive outlays of money.

Bonsai tours

Specialist tours and holidays are becoming increasingly popular, and bonsai is no exception. Japan has always been a very popular destination for the bonsai enthusiast. Tours to China are also increasing in popularity.

The way ahead

One of the objectives of this book has been to inspire you to create good bonsai in a variety of ways. There are no hard and fast rules in bonsai, and certainly no one can claim to know all the secrets; local conditions will vary, and you will have to adapt and improvize in order to achieve the desired results. However, what I have attempted to do, is to broaden your vision of bonsai, and thus enable you to see the potential for creating bonsai from everyday material.

To progress in bonsai: keep an open mind; do not allow yourself to become stale through repetition; and above all, enjoy every moment of your bonsai activities. I would like to leave you with a thought which was passed on to me by an Indian bonsai enthusiast, and which I have found very helpful: "Who is wise? A man who can learn from others."

Bonsai
tools

In comparison with many hobbies, bonsai does not demand much in the way of specialist equipment. There are no more than perhaps five basic tools which are essential: shears, special branch cutters, scissors, a cultivator, or rake, and a turntable. Even the specialist tools are, in the main, simple hand tools – various types of pruners, scissors, and cutters. You do not need to use power tools, such as saws, chisels and routers, although they will save time and effort.

It is important to look after your tools: cutting edges should be kept sharp; tools should be cleaned and dried each day after use; and smearing a little oil over each cutting surface before putting the tool away will help to prevent rusting. Although specialist tools are useful they are by no means indispensable. After all, the ancient Chinese and Japanese artists only had scissors and knives to create their masterpieces. A great deal can be achieved by improvisation.

Only three of the basic tools shown are specially made for bonsai – (bottom left) scissors used for cutting roots during repotting, long-handled scissors for penetrating deep into the branch structure, and branch cutters (this particular type is known as a "wen" cutter). The shears, pruning saw, and small hand cultivator can be obtained from any gardening store; the plastic mesh for covering the drainage holes of bonsai pots is ordinary plastic greenhouse shade netting; and the aluminum wire can be purchased from an electrical or hardware store.

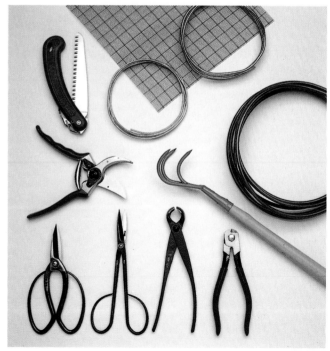

Right A small selection of the chisels, cutters, and scissors used for pruning and cutting: the chisels (top left) each have a special use; the two large cutters (top right) are for removing branches; the stainless steel cultivator is for teasing out roots; the vast array of scissors are for trimming twigs, leaves, and roots. **Below** A selection of carving tools comprising traditional hand chisels, and power tools, such as a chain saw, an electric drill with grinding and polishing attachments, and an electric drill with a flexible drive attachment, used with small router bits.

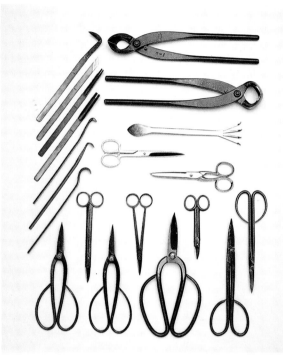

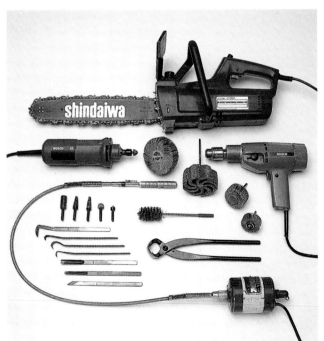

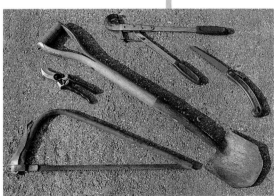

Above Some of the basic tools which are indispensable for any collecting expedition: a collapsible spade for digging up trees and severing roots; an array of sharp saws for cutting down taller trees and sawing through thicker roots; short and longhandled shears for removing branches.

Index

Acknowledgments

I must say that I have thoroughly enjoyed writing this, my second book on bonsai. Unlike the first one, this has been written to a more generous deadline and, to that extent, has been more relaxing. The photographic sessions have also been better planned. It has been a great pleasure to work once again with photographer Larry Bray. His photographs certainly match those of the best Japanese manuals. He probably now knows as much about bonsai as any bonsai enthusiast in the UK. The same perhaps is also true of Sally MacEachern, the senior editor at The Paul Press.

A special word of thanks to Dr. J. Hey, Chairman of the Zen Foundation in the UK for his helpful advice on the influence of Zen on bonsai aesthetics. Thanks also to my good friend Ken Leaver for the loan of his air layerings.

Above all I would like to thank my wife Dawn for all the painstaking research and typing of the manuscript which had to be fitted in with all her other business commitments at "Herons Nursery", which she runs.